With Great Hope

With Great Hope

Women of the California Gold Rush

JoAnn Chartier
Chris Enss

TWODOT®

GUILFORD, CONNECTICUT
HELENA, MONTANA
AN IMPRINT OF THE GLOBE PEQUOT PRESS

© 2000 JoAnn Chartier and Chris Enss
All rights reserved. No part of this book may be reproduced or transmitted in
any form by any means, electronic or mechanical, including photography and
recording, or by any information storage and retrieval system, except as may
be expressly permitted by the 1976 Copyright Act or by the publisher.
Requests for permission should be made in writing to The Globe Pequot
Press, P.O. Box 480, Guilford, Connecticut 06437.

Two Dot is a registered trademark of The Globe Pequot Press.

Cover photos courtesy Searls Historical Library, Library of Congress, and
Alaska State Library—Historical Collections

Library of Congress Cataloging-in-Publication Data
Chartier, JoAnn.
    With great hope : women of the California gold rush / JoAnn Chartier, Chris Enss.
       p. cm.
    Includes bibliographical references (p.) and index.
    ISBN 1-56044-888-1 (softcover)
       1. Women pioneers--California--Biography. 2. California--Gold discoveries. 3.
    Frontier and pioneer life--California. 4. California--Biography. I. Enss, Chris, 1961-
    II. Title
    F865.C465 2000
    979.4'04'0820922--dc21
    [B]   99-054899

Manufactured in the United States of America

First Edition/Third Printing

JoAnn Chartier's Dedication

To my children Chris, Mark, Laurie & James

Chris Enss's Dedication

to Virginia Upton
—An Extraordinary History Teacher

Contents

Acknowledgments

Researching the lives of women during the California Gold Rush is rather like searching for gold. Sometimes nuggets of information are easy to find, but more often the value of contributions by women is hidden under the names of husbands, obliquely referred to in biographies of famous figures, or casually mentioned in newspapers.

Searching out these nuggets of information is not an easy task. The authors owe a debt of thanks to the pioneers who began researching HERstory—the female side of history—and to the libraries and historical societies providing clues to rich mines of information. A visit to gold rush museums and archives is well worth the time.

Sometimes astonishing historical displays may be found in the most unexpected places. One of those places is the University of California School of Dentistry, where Nellie Chapman's equipment is set up in the lobby of the clinic. Particular thanks to Dr. Troy E. Daniels, Associate Dean, Academic Affairs, for recognizing the value of displaying Nellie Chapman's effects and for leaving untouched in her books the small clues to Nellie's life.

Published historical materials are another rich lode to explore when browsing through history. The Huntington Library, for example, published the recollections of Mary Hallock Foote, with an introduction by Rodman Paul, which tells Mary's story in her own words. Repositories like the Huntington provide a rich treasure for the California history explorer.

In Sacramento, the California State Library and its librarians provide excellent assistance amid a wealth of information.

Acknowledgments

Ed Tyson, librarian for the Searls Library and the volunteers at the Doris Foley Library of Historical Research in Nevada City as well as the Grass Valley library staff provided invaluable assistance. Author Peter Palmquist, who unearthed Eliza Withington's marvelous description of how she photographed the countryside, deserves special mention. His books on women photographers are invaluable research tools.

And, for their dedication and guidance on this project, particular thanks to our editors, Charlene Patterson and Megan Hiller.

CALIFORNIA GOLD COUNTRY

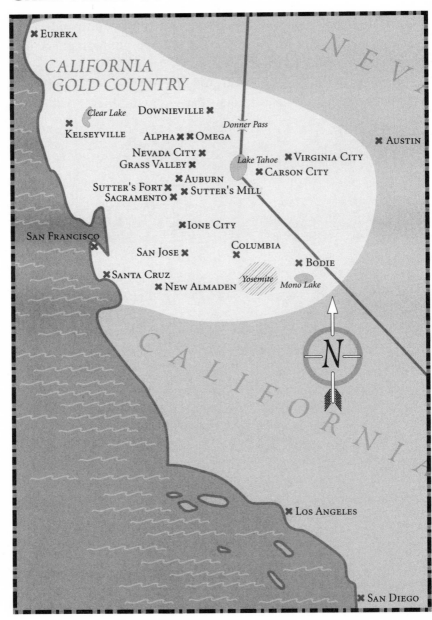

Introduction

The discovery of gold at Sutter's Mill in 1848 became a siren call that many Americans couldn't resist. The pine-covered hills and rock-lined rivers of northern California offered the possibility of sudden wealth and the chance to create a brand new life in a wild, unsettled territory. Enthusiastic young men arrived overland and by sea, intent on picking up a fortune in the nearest stream.

But the story of the early days of California is not just the story of adventurous young men. It is also, and was from the beginning, a story of the women who came with them. These women left home, often either pregnant or with young children, to make a long, dangerous journey through unknown territory.

Only one reason I'd think of uprooting my children and going west . . . the promise of a better life. A chance to be in a place where poor folks can prosper . . .

Susan Frances Lomax
Mother of two, 1849

The trails leading to the California gold fields stretched across rivers, through scorched, lifeless deserts and over the steep Sierra Nevada mountains. The trek was so physically demanding that many believed only men should be allowed to journey west.

Traveling the Rocky Mountains is too rough for the gentler sex. The whole continent of America is not enough to tempt me to consider the danger of taking women into that rugged country.

George Catlin
Trapper, 1850

But thousands of women felt they had enough strength and desire to make it to California. They would find that the trip was indeed strenuous and also filled with unexpected hardships such as food poisoning, animal attacks, and horrendous weather. When they reached the tent cities of the Gold Rush, they found the same primitive conditions they had encountered on the trail, compounded by lawlessness, loneliness, and lack. Nevertheless, the wives and daughters often succeeded at making money in these conditions where their fortune-hunting husbands and fathers failed.

> *There's big talk from the men about finding a fortune. I want for the finer things in life too and I shall have it! Even though folks are against wildcatters being anything other than the male of the species.*
>
> Ethel McCormick
> Wife and mother, 1849

While few women lifted a shovel in search of gold, many won and lost fortunes in other ways.

> *The women of easy virtue here earn a tremendous amount of money. A whole night with one of these ladies costs from two to four hundred dollars. If you ask me they are the real gold rushers. Miners will give up their entire fortune for one night of pleasure and amusement.*
>
> Albert Benard
> Forty-niner, 1851

Contrary to popular belief, all the women of the California Gold Rush did not earn their livings in saloons, gambling halls, or cribs. Some began in these places, but many women of the West found other ways to make a fortune. Some worked tirelessly toward political change for women, and others simply did what women were expected to do during that time, and did it extremely well.

As always occurs to the mind of a woman, I thought of taking in borders. There was a hotel near by and the men that ate there paid a dollar a meal. With my own hands I chopped stakes, drove them into the ground, and set up my table. I bought provisions at a neighboring store and when my husband came back at night, he found twenty miners eating at my table. Each man as he rose put a dollar in my hand and said I might count on him as a permanent customer. I called my hotel El Dorado.

Luzena Stanley Wilson
1850

With Great Hope: Women of the California Gold Rush tells the stories of twelve women—famous, notorious, or unknown—who seized opportunities to take on more than traditional women's roles. Read about Nancy Kelsey, the first white woman to cross the Sierra Nevada, and Nellie Pooler Chapman, the first female registered to practice dentistry in the Far West. *With Great Hope* also tells the stories of women who came to California with great hope but ended up losing their lives there. Read about Juanita, the only woman ever hanged for murder in California, and Eleanora Dumont, a gambler.

All of the women included in this book were part of the California Gold Rush. They provide a sampling of the many women who came west in search of a fortune. Their contributions are varied. Their stories are absolutely compelling.

Nancy Kelsey

Nancy Kelsey

First Woman to Cross the Sierras

We followed the Indian, and he led us along shelves of rock high
in the Sierras, which overhung vast precipices. We all went on foot,
leading our animals. Once, I remember, when I was struggling along
trying to keep my horse from going over, I looked back and saw Missus
Ben Kelsey a little way behind me, with her child in her arms, barefooted,
I think, and leading a horse . . . a sight I shall never forget.

Nicholas Dawson
Bidwell–Bartleson party, 1841

Nancy Kelsey stood on the porch of her rustic home in Jackson County, Missouri, watching her husband load their belongings onto a covered wagon. Soon, the young couple and their one-year-old daughter would be on the way to California. She hated leaving her family behind and she knew the trip west would be difficult, but she believed she could "better endure the hardships of the journey than the anxieties for an absent husband."

Nancy was born in Barren County, Kentucky, in 1823. She married Benjamin L. Kelsey when she was fifteen. She had fallen in love with his restless, adventurous spirit, and from the day the two exchanged vows she could not imagine her life without him. At the age of seventeen, Nancy agreed to follow Benjamin to a strange new land rumored to be a place where a "poor man could prosper."

Nancy, Benjamin, and their daughter, Ann, arrived in Spalding Grove, Kansas just in time to join the first organized group of American settlers travelling to California by land. The train was organized and led by John Bidwell, a New York schoolteacher, and John Bartleson, a land speculator and wagon master.

Nancy's recollections of some of the other members of the Bidwell–Bartleson party and the apprehension she felt about the trip were recorded in the *San Francisco Examiner* in 1893. She described what it was like when the wagon train first set out on its way on May 12, 1841: "A man by the name of Fitzpatrick was our pilot, and we had a priest with us who was bound for the northwest coast to teach the Flathead Indians. We numbered thirty-three all told and I was the only woman. I had a baby to take care of, too."

Nancy was worried for her baby and hoped that she would be able to keep her healthy and out of harm's way. She was terrified that the wagon train might get lost in the wilderness and that everyone might die of starvation. No one in the party was really sure what lay ahead for them. They had no guide and no compass. One pioneer with the train told them he had seen a map showing a great lake with two rivers running out of it clear to the Pacific Ocean. "All we need to do is find the lake and follow the rivers to the sea," he said, "and we'll run into California."

By July, the emigrant party had made it to Fort Laramie, in Wyoming. The party experienced little trouble on the first twelve hundred miles of the trip, but according to Nancy's interview in the *San Francisco Examiner,* the difficulties they had on the trip from Wyoming to California more than made up for it:

> Our first mishap was on the Platte River, where a young man named Dawson was captured by Indians and stripped of his clothing. They let him go then and then followed him so that, without his knowing it, he acted as their guide to our camp. The redskins surrounded our camp and remained all night, but when daylight showed them our strength they went away.

Nancy was frightened by the Indians and stayed close to her husband. Whenever she wanted to turn back, Benjamin would urge her on by quoting the notices about California that he had read in the Western Emigration Society paper. They called California "a land of perennial spring and boundless fertility." Nancy's daydreams about the life they would have there sustained her for a time but eventually her worst fears were realized.

By August, the Bidwell–Bartleson party was completely lost. They knew they were supposed to be near the Humboldt River, but it was nowhere in sight. Food was getting scarce, and the animals became too exhausted to pull the wagons. Still, the party pushed west, abandoning their wagons one by one and slaughtering their oxen for food. Through it all, Nancy never forgot that the Indians were a constant threat:

> We left our wagons and finished our journey on horseback and drove our cattle. I carried my baby in front of me on the horse. At one place the Indians surrounded us, armed with their bows and arrows, but my husband leveled his gun at the chief and made him order his Indians out of arrow range.

On September 7, 1841, the weary group located the Humboldt River, but then could not find the road that would lead from there to the Truckee River. Nancy held her daughter tightly in her arms and desperately tried to shade her from the sun. Her baby was hungry and cried to be fed, but food was again running short. In October, the party killed the last of their oxen. The weather turned cold, and Nancy longed to go back home, but the party continued on until they came face to face with several high peaks.

Later, Nancy recalled the struggle through the jagged mountains that appeared to be "capped with snow, perhaps of a thousand years."

> We crossed the Sierra Nevadas at the head waters of the San Joaquin River. We camped on the summit. It was my eighteenth birthday. We had difficult time to find a way down the mountains. At one time I was left alone for nearly half a day, and as I was afraid of Indians, I sat all the while with my

baby on my lap. It seemed to me while I was there alone that the moaning of the winds through the pines was the loneliest sound I had ever heard.

After exploring the mountainside, Nancy's husband, along with fellow traveler Josiah Beldon, found a place where the party could descend. Benjamin led the party along the steep cliffs and over rough rocks. Nancy remembered the trek as dangerous and one where she almost lost the love of her life.

At one place four pack animals fell over a bluff, and they went so far that we never attempted to recover the packs. We were then out of provisions, having killed and eaten all our cattle. I walked barefooted until my feet were blistered, and lived on roasted acorns for two days. My husband came very near dying with the cramps, and it was suggested to leave him, but I said I never would do that, and we ate a horse and remained over till the next day, when he was able to travel.

Nancy was an inspiration to her fellow travelers. Many of them kept journals in which they wrote about her bravery and made mention of the fact that her baby was never sick a day of the trip. In 1842, Joseph Chiles, one of the members of the party wrote about Nancy's courage and strength: "She bore the fatigues of the journey with so much heroism, patience, and kindness that there still exists a warmth in every heart for the mother and her child."

Nancy Kelsey's pioneering days did not end once she made it over the Sierra Nevada range. She had hoped Benjamin would settle down and build a life for her and daughter Ann, but after five months of being in California, he decided to move the family to Oregon. Nancy didn't want to go, but she was dedicated to her husband. She recalled that the trip to Oregon proved to be even more harrowing than their initial journey west.

We went up the east side of the Sacramento River for about forty miles where we crossed over by swimming our horse and cattle. It was there I witnessed the killing of an Indian. The men were all out trying to drive the stock into the river and I was left alone in the camp, when several nude Indians came in and as I thought they intended to steal I stepped to a tree where the guns were. As they approached me I warned them away.

My husband saw from where he was that Indians were in camp and sent one of the men, whom we called Bear Dawson, to protect me. He was a reckless young man, and as he rode up he ordered the Indians to go, but they drew their bows on him and reversed the order. Then he drew his pistol and killed one of them and the rest fled. The Indian fell within six feet of me.

Benjamin continued his nomadic ways. He and Nancy traveled next from Oregon to the Napa Valley, the San Joaquin plains, and Mendocino. Benjamin left Nancy alone in 1848 to see if there was any truth to the gold rumors. He was gone ten days and brought back one thousand dollars. The next time he went to the mines he took a flock of sheep up for mutton and brought back sixteen thousand dollars. He used the money to buy Nancy, and by this time their two daughters, a lake ranch in a town the couple had helped build called Kelseyville.

Nancy was finally living the good life her husband had promised her, but it was short-lived. Benjamin sold the lake ranch after a few months and took his family down the Humboldt River to be among the first settlers of Eureka and Arcata. Just when Nancy thought they would finally stay put, Benjamin came down with tuberculosis, and they were compelled to travel to a dryer location for his health. Nancy later told the *San Francisco Examiner* about their stay in Texas and the trouble that they encountered:

In 1861 we were attacked by Comanche Indians. The men were out hunting turkeys, and a neighboring woman and her children and I and mine were there alone. I discovered the Indians approaching our camp, which was situated in a brushy place. I loaded the guns we had and suggested that all hide themselves. The two oldest girls ran and hid and a sixteen-year-old boy went along to a hiding-place. The women and the smaller children secreted ourselves in a small cave.

They succeeded in catching my girl because her dress got tangled in the brush. She was twelve years old. We found her the next day, but oh, the anxiety I felt during that long night. Yes, we found her, and my anguish was horrible when I discovered that she had been scalped and was partially deranged. My husband and seventeen men followed the Indians three hundred miles, but never caught up with them.

In 1864, Nancy followed Benjamin back to California. He built her a cabin high up in the Cuyama Mountains in San Diego. He died in Los Angeles in 1888. Her daughter who was scalped died in Fresno at the age of eighteen as a result of her earlier injuries. Nancy died of cancer in 1896. History records that she was the first white woman to cross the Sierra Nevada, but she remembered many more eventful experiences: "I have enjoyed riches and suffered the pangs of poverty. I have seen U.S. Grant when he was little known; I have baked bread for General Fremont and talked to Kit Carson. I have run from bear and killed most all other kinds of smaller game."

Nancy Kelsey's grave in Santa Barbara is marked by a rock. The simple inscription on it reads, Kelsey.

Robert Holmes/Cal Tour

Pioneer Monument.
Though this monument honors all pioneers who traveled the California Trail, it is widely thought of as a tribute to the Donner Party.

Mary Graves

DONNER PARTY HERO

*I wish I could cry but I cannot. If I could forget the tragedy perhaps I
would know how to cry again.*

Mary Graves

*I*f Mary Graves had stayed in Marshall County, Illinois, she
might have married the boy next door, taught students to read
in a one-room schoolhouse, and lived out her days watching
her children and grandchildren grow up on the family farm. Her
life, however, took a different course when her family joined the
Donner Party in 1846 and headed west.

Mary was nineteen when her father, Franklin, made the decision to move his family to California. The wagon train the Graves
joined was organized by George and Jacob Donner and James Reed
and their families. The initial group set out from Springfield, Illinois in April and was joined by additional members when it reached
Independence, Missouri. Franklin and Elizabeth Graves and their
nine children joined the Donner Party in August at Fort Bridger,
Wyoming, with their belongings piled in three large wagons.

Mary was excited about the journey. She had no doubt heard
stories of this golden land of opportunity and couldn't wait to see
its riches for herself. She knew her family might experience difficulties getting there but that had not put a damper on her gleeful
spirit. She didn't care that the trail was treacherous, and she wasn't
afraid of the Indians that guarded the way. She placed all her faith
in God and her father to get her and her family to their new home
safely.

Historical records state that Mary was a beautiful young lady with dark eyes and long, wavy black hair. She carried her slender, five-foot, seven-inch frame with grace. Her complexion was creamy olive. She captured the attention of many of the twenty-two single men in the party, but she was engaged to John Snyder, the driver of one of her father's teams.

Her beauty even drew the attention of the Sioux Indians the party encountered in their travels. Noah James, a member of the Donner Party, noted:

> Mary and her brother William were riding on horseback at the rear of the train when a band of Sioux approached the two. The Indians were enamored with Mary and offered to buy her from her brother. William declined the offer. The Indians seized the bridle of Mary's horse and attempted to carry her away captive. The bridle was promptly dropped when William leveled his rifle at the men.

On October 5, John Snyder and Milton Elliott, another driver, exchanged heated words over whose team of oxen could pull a load up a steep hill. John's and Milton's teams got tangled up as they raced each other to the top of the hill. John was furious and started cussing at Milton and beating his livestock with a whip-stock. James Reed stepped in and tried to calm him down. John thought James was threatening him, and he jumped off his wagon and beat James over the head with the butt end of his heavy whip-stock while Mary looked on in horror. When James Reed managed to stand up and wipe the blood from his eyes, his wife ran over to help him, and John hit her over the head too. James quickly pulled out a knife and stabbed John. Mary's intended died fifteen minutes later. The stunned onlookers were outraged. They wanted to hang James. Mary was asked to sit in judgement of him, but she refused. James was banished from the group.

The gleam in Mary's eyes had started to fade. The journey west was grueling. In addition to having battled the heat and rough terrain, the party had taken a "shortcut" to California that actually took them several hundred miles out of their way. Lack of water and a variety of petty arguments, like the one between John, Milton, and James, created strife among the party members. Their food was running low and many of their oxen and horses had been stolen by Indians. The trip was no longer an exciting adventure but a harsh, seemingly endless trek.

Mary and the others finally reached the Sierra Nevada Mountains on October 28. Generally, this final pass brought joy to weary emigrants. It brought terror and dismay to the Donner Party. They could see dark skies up ahead. Soon these winter storm clouds dumped six inches of snow on the travelers. They were trapped; the snow prevented them from going any farther.

The emigrants quickly built crude cabins near a lake to protect them from the cold. Mary's family shared their tiny makeshift home with another large family in the party. Food was scarce. Time passed and the snow continued to fall.

By mid-December, Mary's father and Charles Stanton realized they would have to organize a team and go for help. Fifteen members of the group, including Mary, her father, her sister, her brother-in-law, and two Indian guides volunteered to be a part of the party and make their way over the summit to Sutter's Fort.

Wearing snowshoes made from oxbows and cowhide and carrying enough provisions to last them six days, the "Forlorn Hope" party set off. They soon encountered snowdrifts that varied in depth from twelve to sixty feet. Mary Graves trudged through the thick blanket of white with all the strength she had. In a December 1846 diary entry, she wrote:

> We had a very slavish day's travel, climbing the divide. Nothing of interest occurred until reaching the summit. The scenery was too grand for me to pass without notice, the changes being so great; walking now on loose snow, and now stepping on hard, slick rock a number of hundred yards in length. Being a little in the rear of the party, I had a chance to

observe the company ahead, trudging along with packs on their back. It reminded me of some Norwegian fur company among the icebergs. I do remember a remark one of the company made here, that we were about as near heaven as we could get.

Generally, the fifteen traveled without saying a word, their eyes fixed on the ground. The fatigue and dazzling sunlight made some of them, such as Charles Stanton, snow-blind. Every day, Charles fell further and further behind the others. On the third day, Charles staggered into camp long after the others had finished their meager meal. He never complained but struggled daily to keep pace with the others. Mary's heart broke for him.

On the fifth morning, the members of the Forlorn Hope set out, leaving Charles behind at the smoldering campfire, smoking a cigarette. Mary was worried; she ran back to Charles and asked him if he was coming. "Yes," he replied. "I am coming soon." All day long Mary kept looking back to see if Charles had caught up with the party. By the day's end, she knew he wasn't coming. Indeed, Charles Stanton had died. Later, a relief party returning to the lake came upon Charles's body after losing their way. They noticed that his body was facing east, and they headed in that direction.

Mary's father and two other men were the next to die. Before Franklin Graves passed away, he called his daughters to his side. "You have to do whatever you can to stay alive. Think of your mother and brothers and sisters in the cabin at the lake. If you don't make it to Sutter's Fort, and send help, everyone at the lake will die. I want you to do what you have to . . . Use my flesh to stay alive." The mere thought of doing such a thing made the girls cry, but they knew he was right. They would have to resort to cannibalism to survive.

The remaining eleven members of the Forlorn Hope party sat down in the snow to discuss plans. Mary described in her diary what the party talked about:

We held a consultation, whether to go ahead without provisions, or go back to the cabins, where we must undoubtedly starve. Some of those who had children and families wished to go back, but the two Indians said they would go on to Captain Sutter's. I told them I would go too, for to go back and hear the cries of hunger from my little brothers and sisters was more than I could stand. I would go as far as I could, let the consequences be what they might.

As the party continued on together, another furious storm bombarded the Sierras. More men died and the women were weakening. It had been twelve days since the rescue team had left their loved ones and friends at the cabins. They had walked so many miles that their feet were bleeding. They were starving and cold. Mary's diary described the horror she endured:

Our only chance for camp-fire for the night was to hunt a dead tree of some description, and set fire to it. The hemlock being the best and generally the largest timber, it was our custom to select the driest we could find without leaving our course.

When the fire would reach the top of the tree, the falling limbs would fall all around us and bury themselves in the snow, but we heeded them not. Sometimes the falling, blazing limbs would brush our clothes, but they never hit us; that would have been too lucky a hit. We would sit or lie on the snow, and rest our weary frames. We would sleep, only to dream of something nice to eat, and awake again to disappointment. Such was our sad fate.

One morning Mary and a man named William Eddy struck out on their own to find food. They had gone two miles when they noticed a place where a deer had slept the night before. The two burst into tears at the hope of finding the animal. They dropped to their knees to pray.

When they sighted the buck, William fired his rifle at it. The deer continued running. Mary cried out, "Oh dear God, you have missed it." The deer suddenly dropped down in the snow and the pair raced toward it. William cut a deep V in its throat, and the two fell on the animal and drank the warm blood.

Within a few days, there was nothing left of the deer and starvation again set in. Only five women and two men still remained. The feeble party traveled on day after day. Their strength was almost gone when someone noticed tracks in the snow. "It was human tracks," Mary later said. "Can anyone imagine the joy those footprints gave us? We ran as fast as our strength would carry us."

The group followed the tracks until they came in full view of a Washo Indian camp. The Indian women and children stared in amazement at the skeleton-like figures that came into their camp. They quickly fed the starving group and tended to their battered feet and other wounds. It had been thirty-two days since the party had left the lake.

Mary Graves no longer looked like she did when the journey began. Her high cheekbones were grotesquely prominent and her cheeks were buried deep below them. Her eyes were dim and sunken. Her once-perfect skin now had the appearance of baked leather. With good food and much care, her looks would be restored, but her spirit never would be the same. She had endured a hard trek over the pass to get help for her family and the other starving emigrants, but all she could think about was making sure those back at the lake were saved.

Relief parties from Sutter's Fort rescued Mary's family and the rest of the surviving members of the Donner Party in April. Mary's mother and five-year-old brother had died which left Mary and her sister, Sarah, in charge of the young children.

The forty-six remaining members of the party were escorted to Sutter's Fort. The horrific tales of survival they relayed to the inquisitive people who gathered around them brought tears to their eyes. Mary's once cheerful disposition had now been replaced with a melancholy nature. She thrived on the stories told about her mother in her last days. Mary's mother was praised by the survivors for her charity. She was a generous woman who gave all she had to give. Mary was inspired by her mother's actions, and it spurred her on despite her depression.

Mary married Edward Pyle in May of 1847. The young couple gathered Mary's brothers and sisters and left Sutter's Fort for San Jose. Six months after Mary and her husband exchanged vows, tragedy again struck her life. Her husband was lassoed and dragged to death by a Mexican who buried the body. Mary was devastated. She walked along New Almaden Creek where the murder occurred trying to find a trace of Edward's body. Not long after the crime took place, the suspect was apprehended, and he confessed. He was later hanged for his crime.

Mary later became a teacher, one of the first in the area. In 1851, she married J. T. Clarke, a sheepman, and they settled in White River in Tulare County where they raised seven children. Mary always stayed close to her home. She died in 1891.

Other members of the Donner Party eventually returned to the "place of horrors" as Mary called it, but Mary never did. All she wanted to do was forget the tragedy—something her children and grandchildren said was impossible for her.

LOTTA CRABTREE AS THE MARCHIONESS IN
LITTLE NELL AND THE MARCHIONESS

Lotta Crabtree

Child Star of the Gold Mining Camps

*Our backyard cornered on one facing the street where the
immortal Lotta lived. I was only 13, but for her I felt it a duty
to gather the prettiest rose in the neighborhood every day. I'd wrap
it up carefully and throw it into her backyard after dark. I would
see the Fairy Star the following morning, fondling the flower in
recognition, and all this time we talked only with our eyes.*

J.H.P. Gedge
1860

A little redheaded girl, dressed as a leprechaun, marched past a group of muddy miners into the center of their rustic camp. Her mother helped her onto a stump while a banjo player strummed a tune for the child, who soon began dancing an Irish jig. The delighted forty-niners clapped and cheered the girl on, and she laughed at their enthusiasm. After she finished entertaining the men, they tossed gold nuggets and coins at her feet. She beamed with pride at the applause and her mother collected her earnings and tucked them inside a leather grip. One of the youngest entertainers to travel through the Sierra Mountains in the mid-1800s, Lotta Crabtree's diverse talents and infectious laugh made her a star in Gold Country, as well as the primary breadwinner for her family.

Lotta was born in New York in 1847 and given the name Charlotte Mignon Crabtree. Her parents, John and Mary Ann Crabtree, ran a bookstore. John, a tall man who sported beaver hats, ignored the business and spent much of his time trying to find a shortcut to getting rich, or enjoying "the good life," as he called it, in a saloon. Mary Ann kept the shop afloat, occasionally bringing in money by working as an upholsterer. Her serious, responsible nature was reflected in her manner of dress. She always wore a one-piece, black taffeta, Princess-style frock. She knew almost immediately that she had made a mistake when she married John, but she was determined to stick it out. Her husband was less dedicated to making it work.

John came down with gold fever in 1851 and decided to move west to find his fortune. Little did he know his daughter would soon be bringing in more gold than he could ever dig up. Mary Ann followed her husband to California in 1852. John was supposed to meet his family in San Francisco, but true to his character, he never showed up.

Mary Ann found herself alone in a booming metropolis with no prospects and a child to care for. She sat down on the docks next to the ship that had brought her there to think about what to do. Her situation wasn't unique. Many wives and children were left stranded in Gold Country by their husbands and fathers. A man's desire to strike it rich often overruled his obligation to family. Mary Ann stared down into the happy, smiling face of her daughter and realized she had to make the best of the circumstances. She appealed for help to a few people whom she had befriended on the ship. Mary Ann moved in with some of these generous new friends and tried to build a life for herself and her daughter.

Theatrical shows were very popular in San Francisco. The various playhouses were always filled with bored miners looking to be amused. As the need for entertainment grew, more performers came to town daily. Variety shows sprung up overnight and featured acrobats, singers, and slapstick comedians. Child actors were held in particularly high regard because they reminded the miners of the sons and daughters they had left behind to search for gold.

Mary Ann loved the theater and took Lotta to see the shows as often as she could. Early on in her life, Mary Ann had wanted to be a performer, but she had abandoned that dream to get married. She watched the actors, singers, and dancers with great admiration and kept a close eye on how many people were in the audience. She noticed that the forty-niners were willing to pay handsomely to see the shows and she wanted to get in on the act. It wasn't long before she became friends with a circle of the most popular actors of the nineteenth century. Her plan was to use them to transform her vibrant, talented, bubbly little girl into a star. Mary Ann enrolled Lotta in a dancing class and encouraged her daughter's acting aspirations.

John Crabtree finally contacted his wife in 1853 and begged for her forgiveness. He confessed that he had found nothing but a few flakes of gold while panning in the creek beds around Sutter's Mill. He pleaded with Mary Ann to join him in Grass Valley, California. He had it in his mind to run a boarding house for miners there. Mary Ann reluctantly agreed to follow her husband. She was less than impressed with the gold mining town when she arrived.

Grass Valley was no San Francisco. It had a population of only 3,500. Three hundred were women, and fifteen were school-age children. The town was rustic and lacked many of the opportunities she wanted Lotta to have. She helped John open their second-class, two-story boarding house on Main Street and enrolled Lotta in the only dancing school around. The classes were conducted in the annex of a tavern.

Jared Reynolds was Lotta's dance instructor, and he was quite taken with her abilities. Many of the miners who stopped in the saloon for a drink gathered around to watch her twirl across the tiny stage. Tears would well up in their eyes as they thought of their own children, and they would shower the tot with chunks of gold and other gifts of appreciation.

Half of California's foreign-born population was Irish in the 1850s. Jared Reynolds knew this and made sure that his pupil could dance jigs and reels —dances very popular in Ireland. One day, soon after she had mastered those dances, the dance instructor loaded Lotta in a buggy and—without asking her parents—took off for the gold fields. When she didn't return home after class that evening, Mary Ann and John were frantic. The Crabtree's first child, Harriet, had died in infancy, and this naturally made them very protective of Lotta.

After a few hours, Jared returned the child to her home with news that her dancing was a huge hit with the miners in the hills. He wanted to organize a musical troupe and escort Lotta around the gold fields with them. Mary Ann wasn't in the mood to hear his plan. She was furious with Jared for taking Lotta without permission and reprimanded him for his actions. John thought Jared's idea had promise.

Jared Reynolds wasn't the only one who took a special interest in Lotta. The notorious Lola Montez (see page 109) thought the child had great potential. Lola lived a few doors away from the Crabtrees' hotel, and she spent many hours teaching Lotta some of her dance steps and how to ride a horse. She adored Lotta and let her play in her costumes and dance to her German music box. She pleaded with Mary Ann to let her take the energetic child to Australia with her to tour the country. Mary Ann, who was expecting another child at the time, refused. She was, however, encouraged by Lola's interest in Lotta. She enrolled Lotta in more dance classes and added singing classes to her studies. By the age of ten, Lotta was one of the most talented children in the Gold Country. She had a wonderful voice, a great sense of comic timing, and was a master of dances like the fandango and the Highland fling.

Just when it seemed Lotta's craft was being perfected, John moved his family out of Grass Valley and headed north to a town called Rabbit Creek. After opening up another boarding house, he left his wife and two children to go out on another gold search. Mary Ann was left to handle the business again. She resented cleaning up after unwashed, dirty miners. She knew Lotta was the answer to a better life.

During her stay in Rabbit Creek, Mary Ann met Mart Taylor, a musician and dancer who managed a saloon and crude theater where traveling players often appeared. Mary Ann convinced him to let Lotta perform for his customers. Lotta danced and sang a couple of sentimental ballads. She was a hit and Mart Taylor quickly took her under his supervision. An actor in the audience, Walter

Leman, saw Lotta's performance and was impressed with her skill. He made a note of it in his journal.

> How thou didst squirm and do a walk around and do all with impunity and vim that defied all opposition and criticism. For thou was bright and merry, and everybody loved to see thee, laugh at the capers, enjoy thy fun, and toss into thee lap the coins and nuggets of the land of gold.

Mart Taylor and Mary Ann quickly put together a company of musicians and set off to travel the various mining camps with their pint-sized gold mine. Lotta was well-received wherever the troupe went, and she earned about thirteen dollars a night dancing and singing. However, Lotta's troupe did meet with some difficulties on the road. Highwaymen would lie in wait to steal from the entertainers. One night, the infamous bandit of the Sierras, Black Bart, stopped the group and demanded their money. Lotta's banjo player, Jake Wallace, was petrified and scrawled in his diary what happened after the robber ordered them off their horses. Wallace wrote: "He walked out of the trees over to us. He was a big man dressed in a long coat with a watch chain coming out of the pocket. We waren't what he expected. When he found out we waren't the mail, he let us go. We parted as good friends."

Lotta's father, again, was unable to strike it rich. He joined the troupe and toured with them for a time. He was amazed at the reaction his daughter got in the mining camps. She was greeted by thunderous applause followed by showers of coins and nuggets. He'd not seen that much gold in all the time he had been prospecting. Mary Ann knew that Lotta's act could earn more money in big city theaters. This time it was Mary Ann who decided to move the family—back to San Francisco.

Lotta performed at variety halls and amusement parks and soon became known as the "San Francisco Favorite." She was twelve and the sole supporter of her family, which now included two brothers.

Mary Ann was in charge of every aspect of Lotta's career. She made her costumes, applied her makeup, booked her into the various performance halls, and made sure the schedule allowed for Lotta to take parts in plays at the better theaters in San Francisco. She handled all of Lotta's money as well, insisting on getting Lotta's share after the box office closed each night, rather than wait until the end of the week. She had a mortal fear of theater fires. A theater's gas footlights could, and often did, explode and cause a fire that would consume a building in a matter of minutes.

Lotta was devoted to her mother. Her high spirits and irrepressible good humor on stage reflected Mary Ann's boundless confidence in her. Mary Ann prevented Lotta from having any intimate contacts or lasting friends though. She believed any outside influence would jeopardize the golden treasure she had helped create. Lotta was totally dependent on her mother and that was just the way Mary Ann wanted it.

Under the watchful eye of Mary Ann, Lotta was hustled directly to performances and home again. And, although she was approaching sixteen, there were still no boyfriends. Mary Ann made a habit of intervening and heading off any romance that might come Lotta's way. A supporting player in one of the stage plays Lotta performed in said she was "guarded like an odalisque in a harem." Most people referred to the cheerful Lotta as "Miss Lotta, the Unapproachable." Once, toward evening in the summer, a young man with a horse and carriage called to take her riding. Mary Ann sent him away quickly, but for days afterwards, following dinner, Lotta contrived to sweep the front porch in case he should return. Unhappily, he did not.

Lotta Crabtree was a popular star and in constant demand. By 1863 she was earning more than forty-two thousand dollars a year. Mary Ann was a smart businesswoman and invested her daughter's money in real estate. She walked the streets of the towns Lotta performed in and bought up vacant lots she believed would be highly sought after as the town grew. Lotta had no head for finances and counted on her mother to pay all her bills and support her act.

At the height of Lotta's fame in California, Lotta, Mary Ann, and her brothers, George and John, traveled east. Lotta captured the hearts of theatergoers in New York, Chicago, Boston, and the Midwest. She performed in *Uncle Tom's Cabin* and *Jenny Leatherlungs*. One of her most popular plays was an adaptation of Dickens's *The Old Curiosity Shop* in which Lotta played two different characters. In *The Little Detective* she impersonated six characters. Lotta was fond of portraying young men. She had such a youthful face that she could get away with playing those kinds of roles, but Mary Ann objected. Not only did she think her child should be portraying queens and damsels in distress, but Lotta had an unladylike habit of plunging her hands into the pants of her costumes. Mary Ann sewed the pockets shut on her entire wardrobe.

Her mother's overbearing actions never dampened Lotta's spirits. Lotta was thrilled with the praise she received from the audiences on the East Coast. In a letter to a friend in 1865 she wrote how she felt about the reception she was getting everywhere she performed.

> I'm a continual success wherever I go. In some places I created quite a theatrical furor as they call it. I performed in Buffalo in a play called 'Fanchon'. The people were delighted and the theatre not big enough to hold them . . .Why, friend Billie, your heart would jump for joy to see the respect I am treated with here among the theatre people. I'm a star and that is sufficient, and making a quite a name.

Even in her thirties Lotta always gave the impression of a young girl, never a woman, but a girl who delighted in flouting convention. She wore her skirts shorter than most, smoked thinly-rolled black cigars, and sprinkled her hair with cayenne pepper in order to catch the reflection of the footlights.

By 1870, Lotta was earning eighty thousand dollars a year and was one of the most popular actresses on the American stage. She spent a great deal of the allowance her mother gave her on her family, lavishing them with gold watches, fine clothes, and sending her brothers to the best schools in the country. Mary Ann kept track of every dime Lotta spent and was convinced that if she didn't keep a close eye on her, the very generous Lotta would give away all the money she had.

On one occasion Lotta borrowed a dollar from her business manager, Eddie Dunn. She misplaced the money and then, feeling guilty about it, confessed what she had done to her mother. Mary Ann cornered Dunn and gave him a tongue-lashing. "Mr. Dunn, Miss Lotta told me that you gave her a dollar the other day, a dollar which she promptly lost. Never again give her more than ten cents at one time. She has no knowledge of money, nor has need for it."

Mary Ann was the quintessential stage mother. She was so protective of Lotta and her fortune that she would fight anyone to keep both intact. She once caught her husband stealing coins from the steamer trunk she stored Lotta's earnings in. She was so outraged by his behavior that she had him arrested. Mary Ann felt John's actions would have a negative effect on Lotta's career and agreed not to press charges if he would leave the country. John reluctantly left for England.

When Lotta and the rest of her family went abroad they met up with John in London. While touring Europe, she learned to paint, studied French, and took piano lessons. She drew attention everywhere she went. She would dress in white muslin and blue ribbons to drive a pony cart up and down the streets admiring the scenery.

She returned to America and the theater in 1875 and continued portraying children and younger parts in comical performances. She loved making people laugh and is considered by most historians as one of the theater's first comediennes. Lotta loved animals and when she finally returned to her beloved San Francisco to perform in yet another play, she purchased a fountain at the intersection of Kearney and Market Street and donated it to the city so thirsty horses would have a place to get a drink.

Lotta retired from the theater at the age of forty-five. She was tired and wanted a chance to rest and enjoy the money she had made. She and her mother retreated to a summer cottage on Lake Hopatcong, New Jersey, that she named Attol Tryst. (Attol is Lotta spelled backwards.) It was a gift from mother to daughter but built with Lotta's money. It was one of the most elaborate homes in the area. It had a split-level design and was an odd combination of Queen Anne and Swiss chalet styling. Lotta found life at Lake Hopatcong dull. In an effort to liven things up, she would host extravagant parties, drive horses, and pursue her painting.

Mary Ann Crabtree died in 1905. Lotta was beside herself with grief. Her constant companion and best friend was no longer at her side. Mary Ann didn't leave a will, but Lotta found more than seventy thousand dollars in cash hidden throughout their home. Twenty thousand of that was hidden inside a granite coffeepot. Lotta also found financial statements that showed the amount of money she had earned off the investments her mother had made for her. Mary Ann's investments had brought in more than two million dollars.

Lotta sold the mansion on Lake Hopatcong and purchased the Brewster Home in Boston, where she lived a quiet, almost reclusive, life. The remaining years of her life were spent painting and giving her money away. On many days she could be found on the streets of Boston fitting straw hats for horses to shade them from the heat.

In October 1917, John Barrymore wrote Lotta a letter and asked her to take part in a tribute to the queens of the American stage. She declined the request and chose instead to stay home, dress up in some of her old costumes, and act out favorite roles from the plays she once performed in for some friends who had come to visit.

Lotta Crabtree died of arteriosclerosis in 1924 at the age of seventy-seven. She left her estate, estimated at four million dollars, to veterans, animals, students of music and agriculture, needy children at Christmastime, and needy actors. She was buried next to her mother in Woodlawn Cemetery in New York City.

Eliza Withington

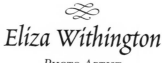

Eliza Withington

PHOTO ARTIST

...secure the Shadows, ere they fade away...

Amador Ledger
1857

*T*here before her was a panoramic view of the snow-capped Sierra peaks—jagged and folded, thrusting upward from steep, forested hills—taller than what they called mountains in the East. The California sky was a blue vault overhead. The sun, she noted, was at the perfect angle to highlight the features of the rugged landscape for her camera.

Eliza Withington pulled away the skirt-tent wrapped around her bulky camera and tripod, reversed the lenses she'd turned into the camera box, reset the screws, and anchored the contraption in the rocky soil of the Amador County foothills. Propping her black linen parasol against the tripod, she carefully unwrapped a sensitized glass plate from the damp towel in which it had been carried to the distant foothills, slipped it into place and exposed the plate.

The camera, covered with one of her heavy, black dress skirts, then became her darkroom. Eliza slipped beneath the dark skirt with water, lamp, and developer, developed the negative, then washed and replaced the glass in the plateholder for a more convenient time to fix and varnish the picture.

Packing up her precious equipment, she scrambled back down the steep, rocky trail to the dusty road, using her cane-headed parasol for a walking stick. There she waited for a fruit wagon to return and carry her back to Ione City and the appointments for portraits at her studio.

Eliza Withington described how she photographed the Sierras in an article for the *Philadelphia Photographer* in 1876. "How a Woman Makes Landscape Photographs" detailed her methods of working in the field. The article provided a complete description of her equipment, how she packed it to survive torturous overland journeys to scenic locations, and how she improvised, using her skirts, shawls, and parasol to process the five-by-eight-inch glass plates in the field.

Eliza loved her work—in particular the time she spent on the road, camping out in the rugged foothills of Amador County. She also loved her family. Born in New York around 1825, Eliza W. Kirby married George Withington in 1845. She had two daughters, Sarah Augusta in 1847 and Eleanor in 1848. George set out for the gold fields in 1849. Eliza, Sarah, and Eleanor followed him to Ione City in 1852. During the overland trip from St. Joseph, Missouri to Dry Creek, California, Eliza and her daughters were the traveling companions of Dr. Fred Bailey and his wife, Mary Stuart Bailey. Traveling overland for six months was difficult, and according to Mrs. Bailey's journal, Eliza's daughter Sarah, then about five years old, had a miserable time of it. Mary wrote that Eliza suffered on her daughter's account and was ill herself with dysentery.

By August, one of a span of horses Eliza was bringing to her husband had been stolen, along with two horses belonging to the Baileys. Although disappointed at the loss, Eliza and the Baileys had to continue on, and on October 5, they finally met up with George. The Withington family moved to a farm and by mid-October, they were busy sending hay and barley to market in Volcano, a nearby town.

In July of 1857, five years after she arrived in the Gold Country, Eliza opened an ambrotype gallery. The opening was advertised in the small Gold Country newspaper, the *Amador Ledger*. According to the paper, the gallery was located on Main Street, at the "first door west of the bridge" in Ione City, a mining town in the foothills of the Sierra, southeast of Sacramento. In the tradition of the day, the advertisement touted all the advantages of the shop, including the skylight, and the business hours, which were Tuesday, Wednesday, Thursday, and Saturday. The advertisement closed with a reminder of the fleeting passage of time and the need to "secure the Shadows, ere they fade away."

Established as a portrait photographer, Eliza Withington was not content with artful poses of families, individuals, and children. Expanding her subject matter, she also recorded the busy mining camp workings and scenic vistas for the stereopticon viewers that were popular at the time. In order to shoot these stereopticon photographs, two photographs were taken with a special camera equipped with lateral twin lenses. When the two pictures were mounted side by side and viewed through the stereopticon, they provided a realistic, seemingly endless, three-dimensional image.

Eliza Withington soon became one of the most well-known female photographers working in Gold Country at a time when the physical effort required to produce photographs was daunting, to say the least. She often used the process called daguerreotype, invented in 1839 by Louis Jacque Daguerre. In this process, used by most commercial photographers in the mid-nineteenth century, the photograph was created with a light-sensitive, silver-coated plate developed by mercury vapor. Equipment was cumbersome and the processing labor-intensive, but many individual and family portraits as well as buildings and natural wonders were captured using this method.

The infant craft of photography sustained many frontier females and provided them with both financial security and independence. Despite the difficulties of this method, which included cumbersome equipment and labor-intensive processing with dangerous chemicals, women ventured into this burgeoning industry. Many began as assistants to their photographer husbands, while others started out mounting photographs. If a woman had to work, it seemed that photography was one of the acceptable occupations.

Another woman photographer who established a permanent presence in Gold Country was Julia Swift Randolph, whose Nevada City gallery operated for thirty-six years. Unlike Eliza

Withington, Julia Swift Randolph spent her time producing portraits exclusively.

Other female photographers traveled extensively taking photographs. The *San Francisco Examiner* featured the unusual lifestyle of Mary Winslow in a story published in March 1895.

> She travels in a buggy, alone, and thinks nothing whatever of driving her own horse over any road where someone else's horse has been driven. She is twenty-five years old, shrewd, self-reliant and not afraid of anything. Her only arms are a revolver and a man's hat, and she goes wherever she pleases. She makes views and outdoor portraits, and they are good ones too.
>
> When the weather grows warm in the spring, she dons a short, plain traveling suit, hitches up her horse and bids farewell to home and friends, to return only when she happens to feel like it. She has been three times to San Jose over three different routes, stopping everywhere on the way. She has been once to Marysville, once to the Yosemite, once to Los Angeles, and has done all the country bordering the San Francisco Bay.
>
> Sometimes she stays four or five weeks in a lively town, where business is good, and at other times she drives, day after day, through mountainous country places where the coyotes stand at the side of the road and look at her in astonishment. When night finds her a long way from any place where she can get a bed and board, she puts on a man's hat and a black alpaca ulster as a sort of disguise for her sex, sees that her revolver is in good working order and feels perfectly at home.

The work and methods of Eliza Withington and other early female photographers are still acclaimed today. The copies of their photographs that exist today provide glimpses of the past and the people who secured a future with their bare hands and the sheer determination to succeed.

Eleanora Dumont's hotel in Nevada City, California

Eleanora Dumont

LADY GAMBLER

The click of the dice, the rattle of the roulette ball, and the slap of
cards greeted my ears as, with my heart beating fast with excitement,
I entered the door of the weather-beaten, two-story frame building
and stepped into the gambling hall. The none too clean looking bar
ran along one wall. Faintly from one of the upstairs rooms I could hear
the gibberish of a drunken man and the high, shrill laughter of a
woman who was quite sober.

Louis Roche
Steamboat Driver, 1871

Dutch Carver, a half-drunk gold miner, burst into
Eleanora Dumont's gambling house and demanded to
see the famous proprietor. "I'm here for a fling at the
cards tonight with your lady boss, Madame Mustache," Carver
told one of the scantily-attired women draped across his arm. He
handed the young lady a silver dollar and smiled confidently. "Now
you take this and buy yourself a drink. Come around after I clean
out the Madame, and maybe we'll do a little celebrating." The
woman laughed in Dutch's face. "I won't hold my breath," she
said.

Eleanora Dumont soon appeared at the gambling table. She
was dressed in a stylish garibaldi blouse and skirt. Her features
were coarse and there was a growth of dark hair on her upper lip.
At one time she had been considered a beautiful woman, but years
of hard frontier living had robbed her of her good looks. It had
not, however, taken away her ability to play poker. She was the

first and best lady card shark in California. Her skills had only enhanced with age.

Eleanora sat down at the table across from Dutch and began shuffling the deck of cards. "What's your preference?" she asked him. Dutch laid a wad of money out on the table in front of him. "I don't care," he said. "I've got more than two hundred dollars. Let's get going now, and I don't want to quit until you've got all my money, or until I've got a considerable amount of yours."

Eleanora told him that she preferred the game *vingt-et-un* (twenty-one or blackjack). The cards were dealt and the game began. In a short hour and a half, Dutch Carver lost his entire bankroll to Eleanora.

When the game ended, the gambler stood up and started to leave the saloon. Eleanora ordered him to sit down and have a drink on the house. He took a place at the bar and the bartender served him a glass of milk. This was the customary course of action at the Twenty-One Club. All losers had to partake. Eleanora believed that "any man silly enough to lose his last cent to a woman deserved a milk diet."

At times, Eleanora could be a tough, shrewd businesswoman, but she also possessed a soft heart. She gave out free meals to miners in need and sometimes gave them a place to stay. She had a weakness for handsome dandies who promised her security and a lifetime of riches. That weakness eventually led to her downfall.

Eleanora Dumont arrived in San Francisco in the early 1850s, and according to historical records, she had one goal in mind. "The western heartthrob I'm after is not a man, but that glittery rock lying among the foothills of the Gold Country." Born in New Orleans in 1829, she was determined to make her mark and fortune in California.

Eleanora opened up her own gambling den in Nevada City, California, in 1854. It was a tasteful establishment furnished with expensive chairs and settees, carpets, and gas chandeliers. Her resort was open twenty-four hours a day, and it soon became the favorite spot for thirsty gold miners and characters passing through the area.

Eleanora created quite a sensation dealing cards. No one had ever seen a successful woman card dealer before. Gaming establishments were dominated by men. Dealing cards and operating a faro table was considered a man's job, and there was not a lot of respectability associated with the position. Gambling and drinking were publicly frowned upon. Some pioneers even wanted playing cards outlawed, believing that the pastime led to idleness. However, not everyone agreed. Many settlers found recreation in a hand of poker or a spin of the roulette wheel. One Gold Country minister was so concerned about the gambling habits of his congregation he implored them to use those diversions "for sauce, but not for meat."

Eleanora's appearance behind the gambling table drew criticism from the respectable women in town. They viewed Eleanora as a threat to their marriages and lifestyle and referred to women like her as "the bad company that drew their men to drink and gamble." Eleanora's talents brought in the customers and earned her a lot of money. Curious gamblers flocked to the saloon to watch the trim beauty with the nimble fingers shuffle the deck. Rival saloons found it necessary to hire women just to keep up with the competition.

Eleanora's success and beauty attracted many young men. His-torical records indicate that several men fell hopelessly in love with the fair Miss Dumont. They proposed marriage and had their hearts broken when she refused. Dell Fallon was one such suitor whose affections she rejected. He popped the question to her one night while sitting across from her at a blackjack table. "Madame Eleanora," he began, "I know I ain't worthy to ask the question. But would you consent to become my wife?" "My friend," Eleanora gen-tly replied, "I am grateful that you hold me in such high regard. But I am not free to follow the dictates of my heart. I must go alone."

Eleanora could have had men by the scores, but her heart was set on just one: Editor Wait of the *Nevada Journal*. She adored him and longed for the respectability he offered. Wait never returned her feelings. He did not want to be involved with someone lacking in social standing. Her broken heart over the matter would never really heal. In order to get through the hurt of his rejection, she set her sights on building a bigger gambling casino on the main street of town.

In less than a year after her arrival in Gold Country, Eleanora had amassed a considerable fortune. Her business continued to grow and she found she needed to take on a partner to assist with the daily operation of the club. She teamed up with a professional gambler from New York named David Tobin. Together they opened a larger establishment where Tobin attended to the games of faro and keno.

Business was good for a couple of years, but by 1856, the gold mines had stopped producing the precious metal and Eleanora and Tobin decided to dissolve their partnership and move on. Madame Dumont had more than financial reasons for wanting to leave Gold Country. When she found out that Editor Wait was sharing his talents with a young woman he had planned to marry, she was devastated. Before she left town, she went to see him at the paper. Tears stood in her eyes as she kissed him lightly on the cheek. "I'm leaving Nevada City to forget," she told him. "I hope you have a good life."

Eleanora took her winnings to the rich gold camps of Columbia, California. She set up her table in the hotel and when profits slowed down, she moved on to yet another mining community. She had a reputation for being honest, generous to the losers, and many times she loaned the miners a few dollars to gamble with.

By the time she reached the age of thirty, her good looks had started to fade. The facial hair that grew under her nose earned her the nickname of Madame Mustache.

She decided to use the money she had earned to get out of the gambling business altogether and buy a cattle ranch near Carson City, Nevada. The work was hard and Eleanora knew next to nothing about animals and even less about ranching. She was lonely, out of her element, and desperate. That's when she met Jack McKnight. "I knew when I met him that he was the answer to my prayers," she confessed. "He was just what I needed and at the right time."

Jack McKnight claimed to be a cattle buyer, and he swept Eleanora off her feet. He was actually a scoundrel who made his living off the misfortunes of others. He was handsome, a smooth talker, and very well dressed. The two married shortly after they met. Eleanora married for love. Jack married for money and property. Eleanora trusted him and turned everything she had over to him.

They had been married less than a month when Jack deserted her, taking all her money with him. He had also sold her ranch and left her with all of his outstanding debts. Eleanora was heartbroken.

Alone and destitute, she was forced to return to the mining camps and take up gambling again. She had been away from the blackjack table for more than a year. She wasn't as good a card player as she once was, but she was still a fascination to most. They would come from miles around to hear her stories and to play a hand with the notorious Madame Mustache.

Eleanora took her blackjack game to many backwater towns across the West. She lost more hands than she won, and she began to earn most of her money as a prostitute and started drinking heavily as a way to deal with her tragic life.

At the age of fifty, she settled in the rough and wicked gold mining town of Bodie, California. Bodie had a reputation for violence. Shootings, stabbings, and thefts took place everyday. The lady gambler, now frequently intoxicated, set up a blackjack table in one of the saloons there. Professional gamblers took Eleanora on, eventually leaving her penniless. But she always had a smile for the men who fleeced her.

One night, after losing yet another hand, she drank down a glass of whiskey and excused herself from the table. The saloon patrons watched her leave the building and stagger off down Main Street.

The following morning Eleanora's dead body was found two miles outside of town. A bottle of poison lay next to her. The sheriff found a crumpled note in her handwriting in her coat pocket. It had not been placed in an envelope for mailing. The ink was splotched with tearstains. The note was addressed to the citizens of Nevada City requesting that they permit her to be buried there—next to her one true love, Editor Wait.

The townspeople were only able to raise enough money to bury Eleanora in the Bodie cemetery. They gave her a proper burial and refused to let her be laid to rest in the outcast cemetery.

Nevada City, California, as it looked in 1852

Luzena Stanley Wilson

PIONEER INNKEEPER

It is the most God forsaken country in the world, not one redeeming
quality except gold....

Mary Jane Megquire
Pioneer, 1850

"*I*'ll give five dollars for one of those biscuits, ma'am." The offer came from a rugged-looking man obviously used to the hardships of living in a gold camp, cooking over an open fire, and eating beans and bacon and not much else.

Busy with supper for her husband and two children, the pioneer woman found it was no problem to add a little more flour and water to the mixing bowl. When the pan full of golden biscuits was pulled from the fire, the miner went on his way, biscuits in hand, and the grateful woman had a shiny five-dollar gold piece.

That gold piece was the beginning of the fortune that Luzena Stanley Wilson created from her way with light biscuits and clean beds.

It was 1849. Luzena, her husband Mason, and their two little boys had just completed a long wagon trek across the country from Missouri to California. Mason was sure they would strike it rich in the gold fields of California. After all, in 1848, James Marshall, the man credited with starting the California Gold Rush, had reached into the American River and picked up nuggets of pure gold with his bare hands. And Marshall was building a sawmill, not looking for gold. Word of his discovery spread like wildfire, sparking dreams of instant riches in adventurous souls all over the world.

Newspapers were full of stories of creeks and rivers shining with treasure just waiting for a man to come along and pick it up. The hazards endured by the rush of gold seekers across the plains and over the rugged mountains were chronicled in Eastern newspapers, but these stories of hardships, disease, and danger didn't stop the tide of argonauts.

Believing they had nothing to lose and a fortune to gain, the Wilson family departed from their log cabin on the Missouri prairie in the spring of 1849 and set out for California. Mason was anxious to get his family to the new territory before all the gold was gone, a fear held in common by many gold seekers. His gold fever escalated when he purchased Joseph Ware's *Emigrant Guide to California*. The book reported that gold lay in the creeks and mountain valleys, ready to be scooped out with just a spoon. Luzena was twenty-nine when she and her husband decided to leave their farm and head toward the setting sun.

The Wilsons, along with thousands of other prairie families, found that seeking the pot of gold at the foot of the rainbow somewhere out west was not easy. Just getting to the gold fields was an often-deadly challenge.

Luzena recalled the terrible journey as "plodding, unvarying monotony, vexations, exhaustions, throbs of hope and depths of despair." Dusty, short-tempered, always tired and with their patience as tattered as their clothing, the Wilson family and thousands like them plodded on and on. They were scorched by heat, enveloped in dust that reddened their eyes and parched their throats, and they were bruised, scratched, and bitten by innumerable insects.

And they were the lucky ones. Grave markers lined the wagon trail west. Burials were common, especially when cholera struck. Some died in battles fought with Native Americans trying to protect their lands, but more succumbed to illness, accidents and to violence among wagon train members. Women died during childbirth along the way, and their children fell before all manner of disease and fatal mishaps.

The glittering dream of instant riches lured them onward.

According to Luzena's recollections, when she and her family arrived in Nevada City, California, a row of canvas tents lined each of the two ravines leading to the tent city, and the gulches were crawling with men panning for gold. Donner Pass, a 7,000-foot barricade of naked rock and fierce storms lay behind, safely crossed before a howling gale swept down on the travelers.

A tent was a luxury they could ill afford, so the Wilsons settled their wagon under some trees and there Luzena set up her primitive household. Women and children were rare in gold camps, and news of the their arrival spread quickly. In many gold camps the sight of a woman or a child recalled the most tender memories for young men who had left family far behind in their quest for riches.

But Luzena and Mason were eager to discover gold. Luzena did not expect to shoulder a pick and shovel, but the startling offer from the burly miner showed her that biscuits and beans might lead her to the goal. This was California, a land named after a mythical Amazon queen. Perhaps the golden legend would bring blessings to an enterprising woman.

During those first few days in the bustling gold camp filled with rowdy young men, Luzena performed the necessary tasks to care for her family as she studied her surroundings. There was little time for chronicling the day's events, but in later reminiscences, she set down the memories of those first few days.

Almost the moment they parked the wagon under a stand of trees, Luzena caught up her two young sons before they could escape her watchful eye and set to work clearing off the dirt of the journey. "I scrubbed those children until my arms ached before I got them back to their natural hue," she recalled later. Of her own appearance, she said she filled her washbasin three times and knew she would not recover her previous looks.

Her face was sunburned, her hands brown and hard. Luzena knew the fashion of the times was for ladies to be soft and white, wearing gloves and hats and carrying parasols to protect their delicate complexions. Her sunbonnet was shabby; the hem of her skirt was ragged above her ankles, her shirtsleeves tattered at the elbow.

The soles of her shoes, she said, had long before parted company from the uppers.

Receiving the huge sum of five dollars in gold for her biscuits that first day must have seemed like an omen of good fortune, and Luzena Wilson was not one to kick opportunity out the door. Like entrepreneurs everywhere, she studied the market and discovered men were paying one dollar for a meal at a nearby hotel. While Mason spent days looking for his strike, Luzena decided to put her skills to work.

Always ready to act on her decisions, she chopped cedar stakes and drove them into the rocky ground in order to set up a table. She bought supplies at a nearby store and cooked a meal big enough to feed a small army.

When Mason plodded wearily "home" from his toil in the creek, he found twenty miners eating at his wife's makeshift dining table. By the time the last man left, paying his dollar and promising he would be a steady customer, Luzena knew she had found her own bonanza.

Six weeks later, Luzena was calculating what to do with the seven hundred dollars she'd saved. Crude as it was, her hotel, as she called it, was paying off. She'd already made some improvements, with a framed roof to cover her cook stove and brush house. An astute woman, Luzena knew that expansion of her business was more likely to support the family than the chances of hitting a big strike.

The town of Nevada was typical of gold camps in the Sierra. Muddy streets, crude shelters ranging from tents to rough-sawn plank buildings, and a large preponderance of drinking establishments constituted civilization.

Among the motley assortment of structures, Luzena's "hotel" did not stand out as anything unusually fine. Nevertheless, she called it El Dorado, after the fabled kingdom in Spanish America supposedly rich in precious metals and jewels, which had lured sixteenth century explorers.

Luzena had high hopes and could already see the benefits of improvement and expansion. She talked Mason into joining her in the business. As the number of customers increased, the size of the establishment grew. First they added rough plank tables to serve even more hungry miners. With the additional gold dust, Luzena could afford to build a bare wooden building.

As more and more gold seekers poured in from all over the world, the business grew. With Mason's help, Luzena served from seventy-five to two hundred boarders at twenty-five dollars a week. Luzena's reputation for providing a good meal and a clean bed drew more and more customers, and she soon expanded her commercial enterprise, hiring cooks and waiters.

It was clear that the best way to strike it rich in a gold camp was to provide the necessities of life to the miners swinging pickaxes and dumping dirt into rockers and gold pans from sunup to sundown looking for a rich strike.

Once again, Luzena considered expansion and decided to risk more of their capital. She and Mason built a store.

After six months of hard work, Luzena's El Dorado Hotel was estimated to be worth ten thousand dollars, and the stock of goods in the new store was worth even more. Again, Luzena's business sense served her well. What was more logical for this enterprising woman, who had made a fortune taking care of a gold miner's needs, than to start a bank? Sure enough, this early capitalist added banking to her list of skills. At ten-percent interest on loans, even she was surprised at her success.

Luzena's kitchen was also her bank vault. In later years she recalled closing the oven door on two milk pans piled high with bags of gold dust. She said she often slept with her mattress lined with riches, estimating she sometimes had as much as $200,000 in gold stashed in her bedroom.

Luzena enjoyed eighteen months of prosperity before she and her family, along with eight thousand other Nevada City residents, were left homeless and virtually destitute.

"Fire! Fire!" The cry echoed through the dark streets, followed by the clang of bells and the racket of pots and pans beating a warning. Snatching up their clothes, the Wilson family and their boarders in the El Dorado dashed through the smoke and flames to escape a blaze that laid waste to the thriving little gold town on the banks of Deer Creek.

Every Gold Rush community, whether a rag city full of tents or a raw pine settlement strung out along a muddy street, was swept by fire at least once in its history. The historic brick buildings with iron shutters survive today because towns were rebuilt to withstand the disaster of a spark, a broken lantern, or an overturned candle. Nevada City burned to the ground several times in the 1800s. Eventually, the town was rebuilt in brick and stone. Permanent brick firehouses for the Pennsylvania and Nevada hose companies were built in 1860 and 1861, providing a central dispatch point for hand-pulled hose carts, but the night that Luzena and her family were routed by the loud clamor of bells, gongs and screams, there was absolutely nothing to do but watch everything burn. Most of the town was destroyed, leaving thousands of people homeless and often penniless as well.

When there was nothing left of their hotel, and the store that held all their riches in the form of supplies had become a pile of smoldering ashes, Mason and Luzena sold their city lot for a few dollars, picked up their children and left Nevada City with only five hundred dollars to show for all their hard work.

Decades later, Luzena talked with an interviewer about those early pioneering years and stated that those hard times were a thing of the past. "The rags and tatters of my first days in California are well nigh forgotten in the ease and plenty of the present," she recalled. Of more concern was the loss of dear old friends, and the memories that went with them to the grave.

From the foot of Coyote Street, near historic Ott's assay office, Nevada City climbs its seven hills with pride in the early pioneers who built in brick after the big fire. Deer Creek bubbles down the draw, luring modern-day gold panners who still manage to find a few bright flecks.

Nothing that Luzena and Mason built remains, but the early work by women like Luzena Stanley Wilson, who helped turn a rough gold camp into a prosperous town that thrives today, is not forgotten.

Nevada City's entire historic district is listed on the National Register, with individual buildings bearing plaques dating the construction and use of the rooms within. Firehouse Number One is a museum, holding the ghosts and memories of times gone by, when the strongest, most adventurous men and women arrived in a wilderness with great hopes for the future.

Some won, some lost, but all added to the heritage shared by their successors, who turned a tent city into a thriving community that today carefully guards its past while looking toward the future.

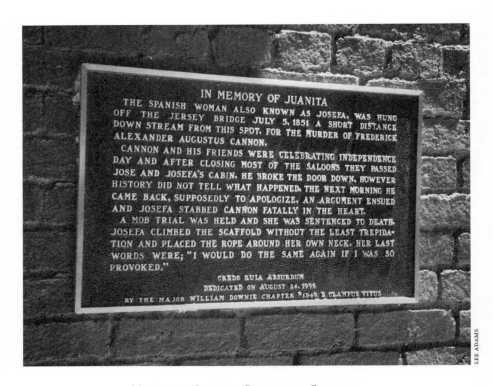

MEMORIAL TO JUANITA IN DOWNIEVILLE, CALIFORNIA

"Juanita"

Old West justice is quick and violent. A couple of nights ago one poor soul was caught sneaking into another man's tent to steal some gold dust. A jury was called on the spot and after a hasty trial, the unhappy victim was adjudged to receive a hundred lashes, have his head shaved, and his ears cut off, and be drummed out of the mines; a sentence which was carried out on the spot.

Robert Buckner
Forty-niner, 1850

*J*uanita slowly walked to the gallows, took the noose in her hands, and adjusted it around her neck. She pulled her long, black hair out from beneath the rope so it could flow freely. A blanket of silence fell over the crowd watching the hanging in Downieville, California, that sunny July afternoon in 1851.

Less than twenty-four hours before, the people in this California Gold Rush town had been celebrating the country's independence. The streets were still lined with bunting and flags. A platform still stood in the center of the town where prominent speakers had given patriotic lectures. There had been bands and parades. Drunken miners had brawled in the streets and bartenders had rolled giant whiskey barrels into tent saloons for everyone to have a drink. It had been a momentous occasion—the first Fourth of July celebration since California had become a state.

Juanita was one of a couple of thousand people who had taken up residence in this pine-covered mountainside burgh, three thousand feet across the upper Yuba River. Downieville was the richest region in Gold Country. Ninety-two thousand dollars worth of gold had been found in the area in the first half of 1850.

No women lived in Downieville in its early days. As time went by and the town grew, some Mexican women drifted into the territory along with other camp followers of varied races. Lonely miners would come from miles around just to look at the women and follow them around.

Juanita probably arrived in Downieville from Sonora, Mexico in the spring of 1850. She was an attractive Hispanic woman with delicate features and passionate black eyes. Her last name was never recorded. Major Downie, the town's founder, described Juanita as "proud and self-possessed, her bearing graceful, almost majestic."

Juanita had a reputation for a hot temper, and her lover, José, was the only one who could calm her down during her fits of rage which were usually brought on by miners making improper advances toward her. She and José had set up house in their small log cabin not far from the Craycroft Saloon where José dealt cards. She loved this quiet simple man and would meet him after work every night. The two would walk home together holding hands in the moonlight. They were happy, but on the morning of July 5, 1851, their lives were turned upside down.

The town's Fourth of July festivities had spilled over into the early hours of the next day. Thousands of intoxicated miners still staggered through the streets, shouting and singing. Fred Cannon, one of Downieville's most popular citizens, made his way down the moonlit street with a couple of his friends, Charley Getzler and Ted Lawson. The three were singing loudly and marching up and down the board sidewalks. Fred was a born leader, ruggedly handsome and chauvinistic. He was good at telling jokes and at impersonations. Everyone liked him. Everyone, that is, except for Juanita.

A young Mexican boy had warned Juanita that he'd heard several men talking about wanting to get into Juanita's house and sleep with her. Juanita suspected that Fred Cannon was one of these men. He was a crude man who hated Mexicans and the Chinese in the area. She kept the door of her cabin locked at night because she was afraid of Fred.

Fred, Charley, and Ted walked down the street until they reached Juanita's home. Fred lost his balance and fell against her door, ripping it from its leather hinges and throwing him onto the floor inside. The loud crash startled Juanita and she jumped up from her bed. "He's come to get me," she thought. Fred laughed and managed to get on his feet again but not before picking up one of Juanita's scarves and tying it around his neck. He smiled at her and she watched him and his friends struggle to put the door back in place and then stagger off down the street like nothing at all had happened.

When José got home Juanita told him what had happened. He inspected the damage to the door and promised her that he would speak with Fred when the sun was up. At seven the next morning, José reluctantly confronted Fred and his friends about the incident. "Señor Cannon, you must pay me for my door you busted down last night." Fred was furious at José's request. "What do you mean 'busted down', Mex? That door a yours would fall down if anyone coughed on it. You come over there with me an jus' show me all the damage I did."

The men made their way to the cabin and when they got there, Juanita was waiting for them. She was enraged and yelling at Fred in Spanish. "Take it easy," he told her. "Why make such a fuss over a little thing like this?" Juanita continued screaming at him and a small crowd began to gather. José suddenly slipped his hand inside his pocket. "Don't you pull a knife on us, Mex" snarled Ted, "or I'll knock your damned head off." José explained, "No knife. Just pay me something for my broken door."

Fred started losing his patience with the situation. "I've got no more time to argue about this. I got better things to do." Fred raised his fist as if to strike José, but the small Mexican protested that he didn't want to fight since Fred was much larger than he was. Juanita pushed herself between the two men, still speaking rapidly in Spanish. She dared Fred to hit her. Jose grabbed her by the arm and pulled her toward the door. "That's right," Fred said to José. "Take your whore inside and shut her up."

José wrestled with Juanita and pulled her inside the cabin. Her anger was now at a fever pitch. "I am not a whore!" she shouted. "Don't you dare call me bad names. Come inside my house and call me that." Fred took a step closer to the doorway. Juanita suddenly picked up a knife from a table just inside the door and plunged it into Fred's chest. He fell backwards into Ted's arms. "That bitch stabbed me." His knees buckled and he collapsed. Juanita stood for a few moments staring at the crimson stain on Fred's shirt. She was horrified. She screamed and fled down the street in hysterics. José and several other witnesses of the stabbing hurried off after her.

Fred Cannon's dead body was laid out in one of the tent saloons for everyone to see. The crowd was inflamed at the sight. An angry mob began to form and they demanded that Juanita and José be lynched.

José found Juanita and the two hid out in the Craycroft Saloon. From the street they heard the ugly crowd shouting, "Hang them!" A group of enraged miners burst into the tavern, found the pair, and hustled them to the town plaza and up onto the platform where the day before speakers had stood making stirring speeches about the country's independence. The mob wanted to hang the pair on the spot, but more levelheaded citizens convinced them to give the accused a fair trial. One of the crowd's leaders jumped up onto the platform and shouted, "We'll give 'em a fair trial first . . . and then we'll hang 'em."

Just two hours after Juanita killed Fred Cannon, the crowd organized a mock trial. A judge and twelve jurors were selected. William Spear was chosen to be the prosecutor. Two lawyers, listed only in the history books as Pickett and Brocklebank, were appointed defense counsel. From the platform Juanita strained her eyes, trying to see if there were any women among the spectators, but there were not any in sight.

The judge called the make-believe trial into session. One by one, Fred Cannon's friends and eyewitnesses took the stand to testify against Juanita. Once the prosecution was through presenting its case, Pickett asked if the accused could make a statement in their defense. José was the first to speak and he told the onlookers everything that had happened, including the names Fred called Juanita, a point that was left out of the other witnesses' testimony. Then it was Juanita's turn.

A hush fell over the crowd as she stepped forward to tell her side of the story. She wiped a tear off her cheek as she searched the mob for a friendly face. "First," asked Judge Rose, "how well did you know the deceased?" "Only slightly," she answered. "He wanted me to have sex with him once. I said no, that I had my man." Juanita sadly looked over at José and he forced a smile.

Judge Rose instructed Juanita to continue on with her testimony. She told the jeering crowd everything that happened leading up to the stabbing. "I took the knife to defend myself," she added. "I was frightened of him so I fastened the door and took my knife to bed with me. I told Cannon that was no place to call me bad names, to come in and call me so and as he was coming in I stabbed him."

The mood in the crowd grew uglier when she admitted what she did. They shouted again for Juanita to be hung. Judge Rose adjourned the trial until half-past one o'clock so the defense might be able to put together additional testimony.

During the recess the mob paraded through the tent saloon to get another look at Fred's body. They didn't need another reason to get stirred up, but they got one anyway. The saloonkeeper unbuttoned Fred's red flannel shirt so everyone could plainly see the wound in his chest.

By the time the trial resumed, Juanita and José's attorneys had found two witnesses to testify on Juanita's behalf. Mister McMurray (no first name recorded) told the mock court he saw Fred stagger, but he didn't see the actual stabbing. He also told them that he did hear Fred call Juanita a whore. Doctor Cyrus D. Aiken was the final witness and what he had to say shocked the crowd. "Juanita is pregnant," he announced. "I estimate that she's about three months along. If she is hanged, two lives would be taken. The court would do well to consider this before acting rashly."

The hostile crowd rushed the platform and insisted it was a trick. They demanded that Doctor Aiken now be lynched alongside Juanita. Judge Rose tried to calm the lynch-mad mob by promising to have Juanita examined by three other physicians in town. A pair of guards hauled Juanita off to a nearby shack where the doctors looked her over. They found no evidence of pregnancy. The crowd roared with approval when they heard this. The testimony ended and the Judge sent the jury off to reach a decision. They were back in fifteen minutes. Foreman Amos L. Brown read their verdict to the crowd: "The jury finds that the woman, Juanita, is guilty of the murder of Frederick Cannon, and that she suffer death in two hours. The man José is found not guilty, but the jury earnestly request that Judge Rose advise him to leave the town within twenty-four hours."

Juanita stared blankly out at the cheering mob. She didn't cry or break down. There were no hysterics, just an eerie calm. The guards led her off the platform and into a cabin. One of the guards stayed behind with Juanita and the other guard closed and locked the door behind him. The guard watched her drop to her knees to pray and make her peace with God. He reported that she stopped only when José came in to tell her good-bye. She burst out into tears and held him close and as tight as she could. He kissed away her tears as they rolled down her cheeks. "You must go," Juanita pleaded. "Go quickly and please don't look back."

Moments later the guards escorted Juanita out of the cabin and to the makeshift gallows at the Jersey Bridge where she would be hung. She gazed up at the blue sky and felt the warm gentle breeze blow across her face. The soft, fluffy clouds off in the distance would be one of the last sights she would see. She shook the hands of a few bystanders and bid each one an "Adios, Señor."

She fought the guards from pinning her arms down to her side after she slipped the noose around her neck. A black cap was placed over her face and then the cords that supported the scaffolding were cut. Juanita hung suspended between the heavens and the earth. Her body slowly twisted and turned. Within seconds, she was dead. It was a little after four o'clock in the afternoon.

The frenzied mob of miners had hung a woman without the constitutional right to a fair trial. The severity of their actions overwhelmed them. The crowd slowly headed off to the saloon to drink off the memory of what they had just done.

In the middle of the night, a few men cut Juanita down. The following day she was buried in one large grave along with Fred Cannon. The news of this miscarriage of justice was printed in newspapers across the state. The July 14, 1851 issue of the *Daily Alta California* reported:

> The occurrence which was published a few days ago, as having taken place at Downieville, proves to be no fiction as several papers supposed. John S. Fowler, Esq., who witnessed the frightful scene, describes the affair as reflecting infinite disgrace upon all engaged in it. The act for which the victim suffered was one entirely justifiable under the provocation. She stabbed a man who persisted in making a disturbance at her house and had greatly outraged her rights. The violent proceedings of an indignant and excited mob led on by the enemies of the unfortunate woman are a blot upon the history of the state. Had she committed a crime of really heinous character, a real American would have revolted at such a course as was pursued toward this friendless and unprotected foreigner. We had hoped the story was fabricated. As it is, the perpetrators of the deed have shamed themselves and their race. The Mexican woman is said to have borne herself with the utmost of fortitude and composure through the fearful ordeal, meeting her fate without flinching.

A plaque commemorating this terrible event is located a few feet away from where Juanita was lynched. It reads "In Memory of Juanita" and briefly tells the story of what happened that day.

ELLEN CLARK SARGENT

Ellen Clark Sargent

GRACIOUS REBEL

*No married woman can convert herself into a feminist knight of the
rueful visage and ride about the country attempting to redress
imaginary wrongs, without leaving her own household in a neglected
condition that must be an eloquent witness against her.*

New York Times
1868

The memory of her arrival in Nevada City, California stayed with Ellen Clark Sargent all her life. Long after she had left Gold Country, she recalled:

> It was on the evening of October 23rd, 1852 that I arrived in Nevada [City], accompanied by my husband. We had traveled by stage since the morning from Sacramento. Our road for the last eight or ten miles was through a forest of trees, mostly pines. The glory of the full moon was shining upon the beautiful hills and trees and everything seemed so quiet and restful that it made a deep impression on me, sentimental if not poetical, never to be forgotten.

In the newly formed state of California, shaped by men and women who had endured unbelievable hardships to cross the plains, Ellen saw an opportunity to gain something she passionately wanted—the right to vote.

Despite defeat after defeat, she never gave up.

Ellen Clark and Aaron Augustus Sargent fell in love in

Newburyport, Massachusetts, when they were in their teens. Both taught Sunday School in the Methodist Church. Upon their engagement, Aaron promised to devote his life to being a good husband and making their life a happy one. But several years passed before he had a chance to make good on that promise.

In 1847, Aaron left Ellen in Newburyport to go to Philadelphia, where he worked as a printer. His interest in politics intensified with the new friends he made. Aaron, an ardent opponent of slavery, closely followed arguments of free-soilers and antislavery forces.

He worked as a print compositor and as a newspaper writer. However, the trade paid poorly. With word of the gold strike in California, Aaron borrowed $125 from his uncle and sailed from Baltimore on February 3, 1849, leaving Ellen with a promise to return and make her his wife.

Aaron arrived in the gold camp called Nevada in 1849 and was moderately successful in his search for gold. He then became a partner with several others in the *Nevada Journal* newspaper. But with a promise to keep, Aaron obtained the help of a friend and built a small frame house near the corner of Broad and Bennet Streets— right in the center of town. In January 1852, he returned to Newburyport to claim his bride. Aaron and Ellen were married on March 15 and returned to Nevada City in October of that year.

Ellen Sargent had no notion of the home she would find, but she was agreeably surprised. She later wrote an account of her arrival in Nevada City:

> My good husband had before my arrival provided for me a one story house of four rooms including a good sized pantry where he had already stored a bag of flour, a couple of pumpkins and various other edibles ready for use, so that I was reminded by them of a part of the prayer of the minister who had married us, seven months before, in far away Massachusetts. He prayed that we might be blessed in basket and in store. It looked like we should be.

Ellen set up housekeeping in a town where the cost of everything was astonishing. Eggs sold for three dollars a dozen, chickens
for five dollars apiece.

"It did not take long for thrifty housewives to make a very good
sweet cake, corn bread, and puddings without eggs," she wrote.
Canned chicken and turkey were substituted for fresh, and women
making homes in the gold camps used dried apples as well as dried
fish. Beans and salt pork were plentiful. Eggs, fresh meat, even veg-
etables were in short supply, and very costly, but another commod-
ity was not. In 1853, California received, and presumably drank,
20,000 barrels of whiskey; 400 barrels of rum; 9,000 casks, 13,000
barrels, 2,600 kegs and 6,000 cases of brandy; 34,000 casks, 13,000
barrels, 23,000 cases and boxes of beer; and 5,000 casks, 6,000 barrels, 5,000 kegs, 8,000 cases and 1,600 packages of unspecified li-
quors.

Despite the preponderance of saloons and the raw nature of the
town, Ellen loved her little home. Her one frustration with housekeeping was in sharing space with the other tenants of the house—
the four-footed ones. The ceilings were covered in muslin, which
easily betrayed the presence of large sized rats. "We did not like
their hills and dales, nor the coloring of their landscapes, but they
were not less happy on that account, if we may judge by the oft-
repeated quadruple swellings downward which were visible as they
scampered like mad across the floor."

While Ellen was creating a comfortable home, her husband was
equally busy, vigorously arguing the political campaign of 1853 in
his newspaper, the *Nevada Journal*. Aaron favored the policies of
the Whigs, an early Republican-style party. An opposing point of
view was enthusiastically espoused by the *Young America*, which
heralded the views of Democrats.

Ellen worried in 1853 when the printed attacks on her husband became so heated he expected to be challenged to a duel.
However, a friend, Judge David S. Belden, came to Aaron's defense before a challenge was issued. Editor R. A. Davridge of the
rival newspaper, *Young America*, was threatening to shoot Aaron

because of his strong political views. A crowd gathered. Judge Belden stepped in, drew his pistol, and announced he wanted to give a demonstration of his shooting skills. Using cards as targets, Belden shot rapidly until the gun was empty, hitting a card with each shot.

He then announced he'd be happy to talk to anyone who didn't like Aaron Sargent, a man who had a family which he himself did not, and thus had nothing to lose if the discussion ended in an exchange of bullets. No one accepted.

In 1854, Aaron Sargent began the study of law. He studied alone and, in August of 1854, was admitted to the Bar of the District Court. He later served as District Attorney and was the first resident of the county elected to the House of Representatives, serving three terms. He was also the first elected to the Senate and the only Nevada County resident to be appointed minister to Germany.

While her husband made his mark in the political world, Ellen Sargent was raising their two children and building her own quiet legend. In addition to founding the first women's suffrage group in Nevada City in 1869, she served as president of similar organizations and presided at conventions called to gather women together to encourage them to continue the fight for the right to vote.

Fiery abolitionist and early feminist Susan B. Anthony visited the Sargent home in 1871. As a young Quaker, Susan Anthony had worked in the antislavery movement until passage of the Fourteenth Amendment in 1863 banned slavery in the United States. With that victory, she turned her attention to another case of unjust treatment in a land where all were said to be created equal—women's rights.

An editorial in the *New York Times* summed up the prevailing view of the "rights" of women at that time.

As for the spinsters, we have often said that every woman has a natural and inalienable right to a good husband and a pretty baby. When, by "proper agitation" (flirting) she has secured this right, she best honors herself and her sex by leaving public affairs behind her and by endeavoring to show how happy she can make the little world of which she has just become the brilliant center.

That editorial by Henry J. Raymond reflected the popular belief that employing her womanly wiles to catch a husband was proper for a female but employing her intelligence to decide civil matters like elections was not.

In a letter to a fellow suffragist in Palo Alto, Ellen reflected on the "great privileges and responsibilities of full American citizenship." She asked,

> Does not that apply to women as well as men? Why cannot women see their low estate in the scale of humanity! And to think they could change it if they would. How their condition argues against their mentality and self respect. Why do they not blush and arise in their might and inaugurate a true republic in keeping with this enlightened age?

When Aaron was elected to the U.S. Senate, the Sargent family moved to Washington D.C. Susan B. Anthony described accompanying the Sargent family on their journey to Washington in 1872. A huge snowfall on New Year's Day 1872 had brought the train to a standstill on the steepest upgrade of the Rockies. The trip from Laramie to Cheyenne, Wyoming, a distance of less than fifty miles, took five days. "Thankfully, the Sargents had brought along extra food and a spirit lamp for making tea," Susan wrote. They served tea and crackers to the nursing mothers on the train and comforted the passengers. However, Ellen herself was soon in need of comfort. "At Cheyenne, young Georgie Sargent got out to explore, slipped on the snow and broke his arm. Watching the painful bonesetting of her little son's arm, Ellen fainted."

Ellen and Susan B. Anthony visited and worked together many times in the nation's capital. In a letter to Mrs. Alice L. Park, a famous campaigner for women's rights, Ellen recalled her life in Washington:

I have many very pleasant memories of the place and the people I have met there. Mr. Sargent and myself, with our family, lived there twelve years. I learned a great deal while there; dined at the White House many times with distinguished people; visited at the Public Buildings; met Miss [Susan] Anthony, [Elizabeth Cady] Stanton, Isabella Beecher Hooker, all the other great lights of those times: love to think it over and appreciate the privilege more as time goes on.

Aaron died in 1887, after serving three terms in the House of Representatives and one in the Senate. He was best known for writing the bill that created the Transcontinental Railroad. After her husband's death, Ellen Sargent continued to work for the rights of women. She was an honorary president of the California Equal Suffrage Association and a board member of the National American Woman Suffrage Association.

In 1900, at the age of seventy-four, she went to court in a test case to protest the payment of property taxes. Her son, George, represented her in court, where she argued that since she was not allowed to vote, it was an instance of taxation without representation. That was, she argued, exactly the claim that started the Revolutionary War which resulted in freedom from British rule. While the Declaration of Independence states that all men are equal, suffragists argued, it was not meant to exclude women.

In the early twentieth century, Ellen was considered an influential pioneer suffragists, giving her time, energy and money to advance the rights of women. She closely followed events in the state and the nation until her death in 1911. Newspapers in San Francisco reported that one thousand people gathered at the Dewey Monument in Union Square to honor her memory. Words of respect from Governor Hiram Johnson, Mayor A. P. McCarthy and other notables were read. Women's rights advocate Mrs. Orlow Black used the occasion to send the call to other women.

The world today has no need of exceptional women. These it has had in Mrs. Sargent and those who worked with her in the suffrage movement. What it needs today is average women to awaken and take up the average work which these heroic women have begun, and when that work is ended, to take up the new work for the betterment of municipal life.

Elizabeth Lowe Watson, president of the California Equal Suffrage Association, said at the memorial service that Ellen Sargent was a staunch friend of the oppressed in all nations and in all walks of life.

She was a firm believer in the principles of pure democracy, in a government of, by and for the people—men and women alike. She was one of the first and foremost to demand and work for enfranchisement of her sex, but her eloquence lay more in deeds than words.

It was her strong conviction that the ballot, in the hands of women, would help to redeem the world.

Women like Ellen Clark Sargent, Susan B. Anthony, Elizabeth Cady Stanton, and Abigail Scott Duniway refused to remain second class citizens. Women finally gained the right to vote August 26, 1920. The Nineteenth Amendment was ratified exactly as Aaron Sargent introduced it forty years before.

The words of Susan B. Anthony's final speech in 1906 to the National American Woman Suffrage Association live on. "The fight must not cease; you must see that it does not stop. Failure is impossible."

NELLIE POOLER CHAPMAN

Nellie Pooler Chapman
DAINTY DENTIST

*My chair is a barrel cut in this wise, with a stick with
headrest attached. The lower half of the barrel stuffed firmly with
pine needles and covered with a strong potato sack over which I
had an elegant cover of striped calico.*

J. Foster Flagg
Forty-niner, Dentist

A groan issued from the adjoining room. Drying her hands on a linen towel, the dentist drew in a deep breath and prepared herself for her patient. Smoothing the apron that covered her diminutive form, Nellie Pooler Chapman walked briskly toward the tray of tools and the lanky miner who waited, hand to jaw in a futile attempt to ease the pain.

With her husband Allen gone to the silver mines in Nevada, Nellie was fully prepared to handle the family dental practice. After all, she'd started learning dentistry immediately after her marriage at the age of fourteen.

Nellie Elizabeth Pooler was born in Norridgewock, Maine, on May 9, 1847. She was married to Dr. Allen Chapman, a bearded dentist of thirty-five, on March 24, 1861. The wedding took place in the home of John and Abigail Williams. This home was called "The Red Castle" because it was made of brick and decorated with white, icicle-type wooden trim. Today it is a bed and breakfast inn and is still called the Red Castle.

Allen Chapman had come to Nevada City from New York and set up his dental practice in April of 1856. When Allen arrived in

Nevada City, he had plenty of cash and some $10,000 worth of dental supplies. A few months after his arrival, his fledgling practice was all but wiped out by fire.

The *Nevada Journal* later related the dire happenings of July 19, 1856.

> At about 1 o'clock P.M. the startling cry of fire! carried men from their stores and dwellings into the streets, and awoke hundreds from reveries of prosperity and happiness to the certainty of poverty and want. The fire broke out in Hughes blacksmith shop on Pine Street between Broad and Spring. The wind, blowing smartly from the west at the time, quickly communicated the flames across the street to the U. S. Hotel. The streets were immediately filled with human beings anxious and willing to risk even life to stay the destroyer, but the rapid progress of the flames soon demonstrated that no earthly power was able to conquer the fiery element.

Few buildings escaped destruction in the blaze, but the brick Kidd–Knox building survived and is still standing today on the corner of Broad Street and Pine. In October 1856, Allen set up a new practice in an office in that building. He continued to practice there for at least ten years, until he built a house across Deer Creek where he and his bride set up a dental office in the parlor.

Dr. Chapman trained Nellie as his assistant. She began her career by applying iodine and pain relievers to his patients. Nellie learned more and more from her husband and soon she knew enough to become a full-fledged dentist. She was recorded as number seventy-nine on the roster of 1879, the first year dentists were required to be registered in the western territories.

Despite the relatively primitive conditions of a California Gold Rush town in the 1850s, Nellie Chapman did not have to depend on liberal amounts of whiskey to dull the pain for her suffering patients. Chloroform and other pain relievers were available to her and touted in professional journals of the day. In 1858, the *Dental Register of the West* reported the discovery of a new anaesthetic.

> A writer in the *Lancet* states that the vapor of turpentine induces anesthesia. The first case in which he employed it was neuralgia of the supra-orbital nerve; the turpentine was sprinkled on a handkerchief, and inhaled in the same manner as chloroform.

It is unknown whether or not Nellie made personal use of the anesthetics available to relieve the pain of labor and delivery of her babies. Her first son, Sargent Allen, was born in 1862, and the second, Chester Warren, was born two years later. Both of her sons later pursued careers in dentistry.

Although Nellie and her husband had a lucrative dental practice in their Sacramento Street home, financial difficulties forced a change. Allen's problems started when loans he had cosigned for friends went unpaid. Some $80,000 was outstanding, and Allen felt obligated by his signature to make restitution of $43,000. Although he was advised to declare bankruptcy to relieve the debt incurred in helping his friends, Allen refused.

By selling everything but the family homestead, he paid off all but $16,000. At that point, he decided to open a second office in Virginia City, Nevada, hoping to make enough money with the two practices to clear the debt. Eventually, with the help of his wife, he made good on his vow and paid off the last of the loans he had cosigned for friends.

While Nellie continued to practice dentistry in Nevada City, Allen took his own dental tools and went to set up and maintain the second practice in the state of Nevada. Despite the difficult trip that required climbing 7,000-foot Donner Pass and traversing the barren desert of Nevada, the Chapman family stayed in close touch. A letter from Allen found tucked into one of Nellie's medical texts discusses the sale of pears and apples the family sent to him in Nevada. Writing to his son, Chester, Allen says the "pears came in all right and as far as I see in good condition." He goes on to tell Chester to "write at once if there are good (underlined twice) Spitzbergs and Baldwins. If you have fine (again, underlined twice) ones say two bushels let me know and I will give the order."

Nellie's contribution to the effort to clear the debts and support the family had to have been considerable. At the time, the Nevada City–Grass Valley area was one of the most prosperous mining regions in California, and, as a result, had a very large population. Nellie's dentistry work was in high demand, and she was also well-known for writing poetry and music. Even as she continued to practice dentistry, she participated in the Shakespeare Club. An accomplished musician, she also wrote music, some of which was published. Nellie and a friend of the family, Edward Mueller, who gave up gold mining to teach music, worked together on musical compositions.

However, Nellie Chapman's active social life did not prevent her from carrying on the dental practice. And, as the family fortune grew, Nellie outfitted her office with the best equipment.

Although they may appear primitive by today's standards, the tools in use during the early days of dentistry did what they were designed to do. Nellie Chapman was a rather petite woman, yet the use of a corkscrew type tool, which wrapped around the tooth, allowed her to wrench it out. Her drills operated through use of a treadle that worked a flywheel, providing the necessary energy to power the drill. In her parlor stood an imposing wooden cabinet the size of a tall, roll-top desk. It was outfitted with shallow drawers for tools as well as cupboards and shelves. The chair for her patients was a grand affair, covered in red velvet and labeled "Imperial Columbia" in gold script. It was fitted with a porcelain bowl on a stand, an aspirator, and a holder for a crystal water glass. It had various levers that allowed it to be tilted for ease of working. Nellie sat beside it on a round stool covered with red and white cut velvet in a floral pattern.

In 1895, while he was still living and running his dental practice in Virginia City, Nellie's husband was injured in an accident.

At the time of the accident, he was suffering from influenza. With his health deteriorating, he returned to Nevada City, then traveled to San Diego, hoping that a milder climate would help him get well. He died in 1897, at the age of seventy-one, and one of Nellie's musical compositions, "Weep Not For Me," was played at his funeral.

Nellie continued to practice dentistry in her Sacramento Street home until her death in 1906. The house still stands on the steep hillside above Deer Creek, a short distance from the location of the first gold strikes in Nevada City.

Her son Chester gave her effects to the School of Dentistry in San Francisco. A glass cabinet contains some of her books, including an 1878 *Gray's Anatomy, Descriptive and Surgical*, an 1875 copy of *The Principles and Practice of Dental Surgery*, and other large, leather-bound volumes containing technical and medical information.

These books perhaps represent both aspects of Nellie Pooler Chapman. Pressed inside one volume are small, dried California poppies. In another is a letter to Chester from his father assuring the young dentist that his mother's letter would follow and a small card from a Nevada City hat maker that reads "Mrs. Lester & Crawford, leading millinery and dry goods house." These small clues provide mute evidence of some of the feminine interests of the young girl who learned dentistry from her husband and who was remembered in the local newspaper for her poetry and musical compositions.

Despite the fact she was the town's only female dentist and the first woman licensed to practice dentistry in the western territories, when she died, the *Daily Union* barely recognized her professional achievements. The obituary lauded her abilities as a writer, composer, and elocutionist, and, in one line, mentioned that she had "practiced dentistry for many years in the city."

MARY HALLOCK FOOTE

Mary Hallock Foote

ILLUSTRATOR AND NOVELIST

Good society was what she missed most. She was not unhappy at all in the hardships; she could take those. She rode across Mexico on a mule ...

Wallace Stegner

Rain dripped steadily from the bare trees outside the dark parlor. The bride stood at the top of the stairs, a red rose sent from her best friend pinned inside her dress. Unveiled, she started down the steps to the man who waited to marry her.

She had resisted his courtship and insisted that marriage did not fit her plans. The young engineer standing at the foot of the staircase had made his own plans. He arrived out of the wild West with a "now or never" declaration. He had taken off his large hooded overcoat, placed his pipe and pistol on the bureau in the room that had belonged to the bride's grandmother, and the quiet force of his intent carried the day.

The bride well knew that the Quaker marriage ceremony puts the responsibility for making the vows directly on those who must keep them. She descended the stairs, catching sight of her parents, a handful of other family members, her best friend's husband, and the man she had finally agreed to marry.

Mary Hallock gripped the arm of Arthur De Wint Foote and stepped up in front of the assembly of Friends, as the Quakers called themselves, to speak those irrevocable vows. She was twenty-nine, with an established career as an illustrator for the best magazines of the day. She had carefully considered what she would give up by taking this step. Arthur was a mining engineer, and his work was in the West. She was an artist, and all her contacts were in Boston and New York. She faced forward with a mixture of anxiety and joy.

The marriage ceremony was considered with misgiving by Arthur's aged father, a staunch Episcopalian who doubted the validity of a wedding without benefit of clergy, but the Quaker marriage contract signed and witnessed under the eyes of God convinced him it would hold.

On February 9, 1876, Mary and Arthur were committed to each other and whatever the future held. "No girl ever wanted less to 'go West' with any man, or ever paid a man a greater compliment by doing so," Mary wrote years later.

Mary Hallock was born on a farm in 1847 in Milton, New York, the youngest daughter of Nathaniel and Ann (Burling) Hallock. All through her childhood, Mary Hallock's family lacked money. But despite the hard life on the worked-out homestead, the tight-knit little Quaker clan gathered together each evening to hear and discuss the latest news. The family was well-connected to the Society of Friends in New York, and speakers from the New York Antislavery Society regularly visited the Hallocks. Fiery abolitionists like Ernestine Rose and Susan B. Anthony brought news of the fight against slavery to the Hallock home, and all the children knew well the state of their country.

Each night Mary's father read the congressional debates and newspaper editorials aloud. A well-read man, his library soon became a source of education for Mary. As her knowledge increased, so too did her talent for drawing.

Following her commencement at seventeen from the Poughkeepsie Female College Seminary, she studied for three years at the Cooper Union Institute School of Design. It was 1864, and Cooper Union was the only place in the United States where a woman could receive an art education.

There she learned one of the most difficult and tedious of artistic processes—wood engraving. Her teacher, William J. Linton, said she was the best wood designer at Cooper Union, and her later works earned praise from a contemporary artist, Joseph Pennell, who declared he thought she was one of the best illustrators of the time.

Mary's art undoubtedly reflected the drama of the 1860s. During the time she was attending classes, three of her young Quaker relatives died fighting in the Civil War. Perhaps it was the emotional reaction to losing members of the family that imbued her work with strength at a time when gently-reared women were expected to do little more than dabble in pale watercolor.

Mary never dabbled at anything. She had set goals and knew exactly how she wanted her life to go. By the age of twenty she had made good progress in her career. That year, 1867, she sold four black and white pictures for a book called *Beyond the Mississippi*, perhaps heralding the future for a young woman content with her life in the artistic and literary circles of New York.

Ten years after she left art school, Mary kept busy illustrating books for a number of publishing houses, and she contributed drawings to such publications as *Harper's Weekly* and *Scribner's Monthly*. Mary's career had hit high gear.

Then, on New Year's Eve, 1874, she fell into conversation with Arthur Foote at a party given by a friend. Mary had retreated to the library to work on a drawing for *Hearth and Home*. As the sun sank over Boston Bay that evening, she rose and walked to the large window. Outside, the spectacular scarlet sunset drenched the frozen, ice-locked bay, dyed the snow-covered roads and frosted the roofs of the houses and wharves with a crimson stain.

Inside, the lamps reflected the interior of the library. Mary saw herself and the room behind her mirrored in the glass. The window also reflected Arthur's strong, quiet face.

He had, she thought, a restful way about him. It reminded her of men who sailed the sea, or horsemen, or farmers in touch with the deep rhythms of the earth.

Picking up her sketching block, she began to draw as they talked. When she at last put aside her pencil, she had drawn the face of the future.

Arthur was nothing like the famous stars of literature that Mary worked with—men like Henry Wadsworth Longfellow and Oliver Wendell Holmes, literary figures who praised her illustrations. Yet Arthur Foote had outstanding credentials of his own. He had worked at Tehachapi Pass and Sutro Tunnel, both difficult jobs for a young civil engineer in the West.

When he was an engineering student at Yale University, an oculist told him his bad vision could not be corrected. Stunned by that diagnosis, he had left the Scientific School two years short of graduation, thinking he would never be able to become an engineer. That doctor was wrong. Two years later, with corrective lenses, Arthur had turned west to seek his fortune, determined to return for the woman he intended to marry.

Although he'd lost two years of his education, he read everything he could get his hands on for every project he did. He worked as an engineer at gold and silver mines in the rugged West. All along, he was plotting the best course for wooing the small, vital, creative woman he'd met on New Year's Eve and then left behind.

He conducted his courtship through letters. Mary wrote back, emphasizing the joys of Eastern society, attempting to make certain her own intentions were clear. She was mature, quite successful and had no intention of giving up a satisfying life.

"In defiance of fate," Mary later admitted, she wrote him of the successes of her career and the direction of her life, "which did not point toward marriage." Arthur Foote was a very determined man. Despite Mary's increasing success, which she shared in vivid detail in letters she sent west, the quiet engineer she'd first sketched in Boston came home to marry her.

In the same year that Custer made his last stand at the Battle of the Little Bighorn, Mary Hallock Foote crossed the continent by train. She did not leave her career behind. With a commission in hand to illustrate a new edition of *The Scarlet Letter,* Mary used as a model for a character in the book the maid who accompanied her on the journey to New Almaden, California.

The western territories provided a perfect backdrop for drawings she sent to Eastern publications. The strength and technical mastery of her woodcuts and ink drawings earned praise when they appeared in volumes like Longfellow's *The Hanging of the Crane* and *The Skeleton in Armor,* and Nathaniel Hawthorne's *The Scarlet Letter.*

Time and time again, it was Mary's talent that saved her small family from going without. Her illustrations of Western scenes were published in magazines owned by the husband of her best friend, Helena DeKay Gilder. It was also the Gilders who published Mary's first short story.

Mary wrote the Gilders a series of letters containing descriptions of the Colorado mining camp where her husband's work had taken them. Richard Watson Gilder, publisher of *Scribner's Monthly,* pieced together some of her descriptions and used them in a couple of articles about the West, clearly hoping to profit from Eastern society's romantic interest in mining camps like Leadville.

Mary was encouraged in her writing by other authors, including Helen Hunt Jackson, who visited the Foote's cabin high in the Rockies in 1879. The result was Mary's first book, *The Led-Horse Claim,* about the silver boom in Colorado. The book was first serialized, then published in a full-length edition.

In 1922, W. A. Rogers, a well-known illustrator, praised her twin talents.

> Somehow she and Owen Wister, two products of the most refined culture of the East, got closer to the rough frontier character than any writers I know, and Mrs. Foote supplemented this with pictures that one feels were made while looking from the rim of some deep canyon or by the light of a lantern in a lonesome cabin.

Mary's devotion to her husband carried her through the adventures of the first years of marriage, when she and Arthur moved about wherever Arthur could find work. Although the couple's finances were several times stretched thin, Mary earned enough to balance out the bottom line. It was not always easy, and she admitted that her pride and her expectations were sometimes hurt.

Gentlemen were expected to provide for their families, but Mary had started married life having to pay her own and the maid's train fare to New Almaden, where Arthur waited. She learned later that his savings had been depleted by his efforts to make his cabin livable for his bride.

Arthur seemed fated to flounder in the boom-or-bust West, in part because of his integrity and high principles. In the early 1890s, some of Arthur's projects failed, the bank that held his funds collapsed during a national bank panic, and his irregular employment led to dire times for the Foote family. During the most difficult years, when Arthur embarked on an irrigation scheme in Idaho that failed, he reportedly drowned his disappointment in the bottle. Mary took the couple's three children and left for a time. It was during this time that she produced a number of stories and books for the commercial market. In her mid-forties, with three children and no dependable income, Mary did what she had to do—she turned out a series of western potboilers that did her literary career no great good but fed and clothed her family.

In less than three years she wrote a novel, five adult tales, two stories for children and two collections of shorter works. Some reviewers believe, and Mary herself admitted, that if her editors had not insisted on a formula they knew would sell, her work would have been much more durable. One of her stories, *Coeur d'Alene,* took as its subject a violent confrontation at an Idaho mine. It was later judged to be anti-union propaganda by one critic, but Mary knew many of the mine owners and engineers in the mining district and followed events closely. In thirteen handwritten pages she explained and justified to her skeptical editor the reasons for using an actual event as the basis for a story. Writing to C. C. Buel, assistant editor at *The Century Magazine,* Mary argued her case:

> I quite appreciate the force of your query as to the possible legal aspects of a story so outspoken as the one about the Coeur d'Alene, but I assure I have borne that point in

mind. The story is pure make up, except where it joins the story of the strike, which is history.

In a subsequent response, Buel wrote a note to his boss, editor R. W. Gilder: "I think Mrs. Foote's accounting of the strike story is satisfactory and promising and that we can accept it conditionally and make an advance if she wishes it. She ought to finish it in the crisp, dramatic style of the half we have seen . . . ."

Mary earned good money for her stories. For example, she was paid $1,000 for "The Last Assembly Ball." She sold serial rights for another story for $2,000. Eleven drawings for "The Harshaw Bride" earned her $470, which she acknowledged in a letter to her editors at *The Century Magazine* as a "monstrous price." Mary lived in times and locations that held great appeal to her audiences. Her drawings and stories provided glimpses of the raw life and often-violent events of the western territories.

Although Mary's fiction won popular favor, it was never considered by critics to be of high literary merit. Her books followed a strict formula and dealt with frontier life as seen through the eyes of a gently-reared female resettled in the West—not a subject considered to be of stirring literary merit as compared to contemporary male writers who depicted the riveting perils and dilemmas faced by their heroes.

Mary's Quaker background was a touchstone all her life, allowing Mary no false modesty. She looked at her own work and knew its worth. Her "potboilers," as she called them, paid the bills, a necessity since her husband's profession often provided an unsteady income at best, and sometimes none at all. Then, in 1895, Arthur became superintendent of the North Star Mine. Settled at last, they stayed in Grass Valley, California for twenty years. "It seemed as if each member of the family had found that elusive angle of repose which one finds and loses from time to time but is always seeking in one way or another," she explained in her reminiscences.

Even at the North Star Mine, with a stable financial base and a real home, Mary continued to write. Harry Tompkins, a friend of

Mary's as well as Arthur's assistant, wrote in the *Idaho Sunday Statesman*:

> The vast amount of work she produced under conditions that would have absorbed all the energies of an ordinary woman, is accounted for by the fact that she seemed not to be dependent upon propitious moods or favorable surroundings, but had the faculty of absorbing herself in artistic or literary work whenever the more pressing claims of family life relaxed.

Family life had always been of primary importance for Mary. Despite the difficulties occasioned by rough living in isolated places, Mary Hallock Foote followed where her husband's career led. Clear-eyed and honest as she was, her reminiscences show her loyalty and admiration for the man who wouldn't take no for an answer. All her life she kept the rose she had worn inside her wedding dress. It was pressed inside a locket holding a picture of Arthur at fourteen, showing, she said, "a daring-eyed little rascal" who would be sure to go someplace far from home.

In 1904, just when things seemed to be settled into that "comfortable angle of repose," tragedy struck. Arthur was aboard a ship, two weeks from docking in San Francisco, when Mary faced her greatest trial yet. Her seventeen-year-old daughter, Agnes, woke up in the middle of the night in extreme pain.

One whole night was wasted, Mary recalled, when Agnes lay in agony but woke no one. The next day the young doctor who'd been called to the Foote home diagnosed acute appendicitis. He was afraid to operate. A surgeon and nurse from San Francisco traveled 150 miles by train to Colfax then came another twenty miles on the midnight special to Grass Valley. The doctor operated on Agnes at the family home located just outside town at the North Shore Mine. The doctor, with two assistants helping, said the operation was "just in time."

Four days later, Agnes died.

Agnes's death drew the Foote family together, and Mary's writing career waned as she devoted much of her energy to her family.

In 1912, Arthur resigned as superintendent of the North Star, leaving the job in the hands of their son, Arthur Burling Foote. The family stayed on in Grass Valley, still tied to the ever deepening mine, and the search for gold.

In 1914, with the world at war, Mary was sixty-seven. She still wore Quaker dress and used "thee" and "thou" in conversation, the speech of Friends. She commented that it was no time for a pacifist old lady to be writing. Nevertheless, she produced three more novels, considered by some critics to be her best.

A Victorian Gentlewoman in The Far West, the published version of Mary's recollections of her life, was written at the urging of family and friends when she was eighty. With an introduction by Rodman Paul, the book provides a detailed account of Mary's life, the inspiration provided by the western territories, and the intense dedication to her family.

Despite her intention as a young woman to stay in the East near family and friends and the great intellectuals and artists of the day, the West laid a claim on Mary Hallock Foote. Everything she wrote included descriptive passages about the land and the effects of the vast workings of nature on men and women.

Her second novel, *John Bowedon's Testimony,* evokes in its final passages how Mary felt about the West's wide-open spaces.

Winds of the great far west, soft, electric and strong, blowing up through gates of the great mountain ranges, over miles of dry savannah, where its playmates are the roving bands of wild horses, and the dust of the trails it weaves into spiral clouds and carries like banners before it. Wind of prophecy and hope, of tireless energy and desire that life shall not satisfy. Who that has heard its call in the desert, or its whisper in the mountain valleys, can resist the longing to follow, to prove the hope, to test the prophecy.

Mary died at the age of ninety. As a bride, she had dreaded leaving the civilized East for the frontier, yet her ashes were returned to Grass Valley's rugged hills.

In 1971, author Wallace Stegner won a Pulitzer Prize for *Angle of Repose,* his novel based on the life of Mary Hallock Foote which made extensive use of her work and her memoirs. Even Stegner's title was taken from the phrase Mary had used when writing about her family settling in at the North Star Mine in Grass Valley. In an interview conducted by Professor Richard Etulain, Stegner summed up his vision of the woman who wrote romances to bolster the family fortunes: "By no means a major figure, she is too honest to be totally lost."

EMMA NEVADA

Emma Nevada

DIVA OF THE DIGGINS

She has the reputation of being only a bravura singer, but believe me, she has remarkable dramatic presence and will go very far!

Guiseppe Verdi
Composer, 1881

*D*oc Wixom lifted his three-year-old daughter and stood her carefully in the middle of a table. Wrapped in an American flag, golden brown ringlets framing her sweet face, Emma Wixom smiled at her audience. The church on the banks of Deer Creek was crowded with miners and merchants, teamsters and saloonkeepers. They were there to benefit a local charity, and the sight of a child symbolized the hopes of the future.

Unafraid of the eager faces crowded around the table, little Emma Wixom knew what was expected of her. She was happy to sing on this lovely morning. She did it all the time, unaccompanied, singing for the pure love of the sound.

That summer day in 1862, in the thriving California Gold Rush town named Nevada, she gave a performance to remember. Inside the Baptist church on the banks of Deer Creek, Emma took a deep breath and released a pure soprano voice that held the audience spellbound. By the time the last note sounded, there was not a dry eye in the house. Brawny, wet-cheeked miners showered her with nuggets of pure gold.

Emma Wixom, the daughter of a country doctor, began a long and illustrious career that day in the church. She would go on to sing opera in Europe and America. She would draw standing-room-only crowds to her performances, but her biggest fans remained the reckless, rugged gold miners who first took a little child into their hearts.

They bestowed various nicknames on her, and the mere mention of the "Queen of the Alpha Diggins," the "Comstock Nightingale," the "Sagebrush Nightingale," or the "International Songbird" brought a fond smile to the face of anyone who'd ever heard her sing. According to critics as well as an adoring public, Emma had a voice of incredible purity. It was her voice that made her fortune, but it was her sweetness that claimed the hearts of everyone from gold miners to gold-crowned royalty.

To the men grubbing for precious metals in California's gold-speckled streams and, later, the silver mines of Nevada, Emma's songs were as marvelous as those of a nightingale. In fact, the girl who started singing by imitating birdsong would one day sing in a command performance for a queen.

The birthplace of Emma Wixom could hardly be less auspicious for someone who would go on to sing in the opulent opera houses of Paris and Rome. She was born in Alpha, California in February 1859, the daughter of a country doctor, William Wallace Wixom, and his wife, Marie. Doc Wixom's practice included treating the ills and injuries of gold miners working the hydraulic diggins of Alpha and Omega, located in the steep Yuba River canyon about fifteen miles east of Nevada City.

In 1859, the year of Emma's birth, miners in the two settlements were working the exposed gravel of an ancient riverbed which had been pushed to the top of the rugged hills during California's violent formation. Prospectors had discovered gold buried in the former channels of ancestral rivers. The only way to get at it was to wash away hundreds of feet of dirt and rock to get at the gold.

Like his father before him, a surgeon for the Union during the Civil War, Doc Wixom practiced medicine within reach of cannons, but in his case an incredible force of water was shot from the cannons in the attack on the hillsides. The force of the water, the shifting slopes, and the rolling boulders were dangerous, and the doctor kept busy tending to the miners' injuries.

Emma grew up skipping and singing her way through the days. She listened to birds, imitating their songs and making up her own. When Emma was three years old, Doc Wixom moved his little family fifteen miles downriver to busy Nevada City, where the population numbered in the thousands. Emma's first public performance in the Baptist church placed her firmly on the path that would lead her to greatness, although no one could have guessed her destiny at that initial appearance.

Emma's sweet voice was acclaimed in Nevada City and her performance in the church mentioned in the local newspaper. However, soon after their arrival, the family moved again, this time to Austin, a small mining settlement and Pony Express stop in central Nevada. Doc Wixom practiced medicine there, and, with the help of his brother, raised thoroughbred horses.

People in Austin learned early of Emma's voice. When she was five, "Little Wixy," as they called her, sang at a concert in Virginia City, Nevada. According to newspapers of the time, the performance showed the early promise that was to result in her later crowning as the "Comstock Nightingale." She sang "John Brown's Body" and "Yankee Doodle" during a parade in 1864, the true soprano notes ringing clear, though she was only six at the time. Emma was eight when her mother died during a trip to visit family in Fenton, Michigan. She and her father drew closer, and from that day forward he became her staunchest supporter no matter how far away her talent carried her.

Always, she sang.

Supported by her father and encouraged by a neighbor, Mrs. Eliza Prisk, Emma took music lessons from a piano teacher in Austin. Her skills and talent grew as she did, and when she'd learned all she could in Austin, a critical decision was made.

Though it was difficult for them to part, Doc Wixom sent Emma to Mills Seminary, now called Mills College, in Oakland, California. She learned four languages and studied music and sang with her classmates. Critics writing in publications at the time mentioned her voice. Secretly, she dreamed of singing to the whole world. The principal of the school, Susan Lincoln Tolman Mills, encouraged that dream and became a strong financial supporter and a woman Emma considered her second mother.

Long after leaving Mills Seminary, after her marriage and the achievement of her dreams in the opera houses of Europe and America, Emma sent a photograph to Mrs. Mills. The inscription said: "To my second mother, to my darling friend and dear teacher, Mrs. C. T. Mills, in loving remembrance of her ever grateful pupil and child, Emma Nevada Palmer." The inscription is dated 1900.

Emma studied and performed during the school terms, but she returned to Austin on long holidays. Whenever she was home, she rode her father's horses, and she sang her songs. The ranch was located at an elevation of almost 6,700 feet, and Emma later credited the dry, penetrating air of the high desert with expanding her lungpower. Every day she practiced musical scales and melodies, once confiding she loved to imitate any bird that had a trill to its song.

Mrs. Mills encouraged Emma, and when she graduated, offered her a position teaching German at the school to beginning language students. The job would allow her to earn money and continue her studies. She wanted that with all her heart, but she knew she had to go home and talk it over with her father.

It wasn't long before the news spread by word of mouth and in the local newspaper that Emma was once again coming home. Austin citizens demanded that she sing.

Tuesday evening, August 8, 1876, at the age of sixteen, Emma sang at Austin's International Hall. The performance earned lyrical praise and was called the best concert in Austin's history. All her life, Emma's voice was admired and complimented but never so heartfelt as praise from a Shoshone Indian chief, as reported in the town newspaper:

> In her hair Emma brings gold from Yuba; Her eyes catch Sierra Brown Hue; Her voice get em silver in Austin; On her

lips she got Reese River dew; So sweetly she sing like one linnet, then like meadowlark trilling along; All clear up in big Smoky Valley; Heap much steam make her pretty song.

Emma's every habit was remarked upon and written about. She was fond of picking wildflowers and weaving them into wreaths that she wore upon her head. The little circles of flowers were soon known as a Wixom halo.

With her father's approval, Emma returned to teach at Mills Seminary and to continue her own studies in music. She met Professor Adrian Ebell, well-known in Eastern literary and music circles. Ebell had come west to organize a branch of the Ebell Society, an organization dedicated to the further study of art, nature, and history. A graduate of Albany Medical College, he had lectured at schools and lyceums on natural science and established a university system for ladies that included tours of the continent.

Ebell was struck by Emma's voice and the knowledge she had acquired at Mills Seminary. He invited her to join a group of young women traveling to Europe for enrichment of their education. It was Emma's big chance, and she knew it. She had the opportunity to study in Vienna with one of the great teachers of the time, Madame Mathilde Marchesi. Mrs. Mills urged her to go.

Faced with an opportunity that was both exciting and frightening, Emma once again returned home to confer with her father. Doc Wixom was not a rich man, but he was very proud of his daughter. He agreed to the trip despite the long separation and the expenses of such a journey.

Before she left for foreign shores, the populace of Austin demanded that she sing for them once more. On March 15, 1877, when she was barely eighteen, International Hall again rang with the Nightingale's song. This was not just a farewell performance; it was also a benefit concert for a miner who had been severely injured in an accident and had to have both feet amputated.

Emma sang the song she later made famous around the world. "Listen To The Mockingbird" might never have gained the popularity it later enjoyed but for the pretty little Comstock Nightingale's favorite rendition.

The performance of that song, and another favorite, "Home, Sweet Home" brought down the house that night in Austin. Rugged miners and hardy farmers who had traveled miles across the Nevada desert to see Little Wixy choked up and let tears fall without restraint.

Before she departed for her trip to Europe, Emma thanked the community in a note published in the *Reese River Reveille*, the town newspaper. After reporting that the concert had raised more than four hundred dollars for the injured miner, she bid the community a fond farewell. "To all my friends let me say goodbye. I trust that you will not forget me, and that the memories which do return will be fond ones. The words 'Home, Sweet Home' that I sang last night came not alone from my lips but were heartfelt."

In April 1877, Emma was one of nineteen girls from California who met many more of Adrian Ebell's students and boarded the steamer *Pomerania*. Nervous and excited, they set out for Europe and the study of art, music, literature, and drama.

Although he was relatively young, Ebell died of heart trouble just as the steamer carrying the party arrived at the Hamburg, Germany port. Ebell's wife decided to go back to America with the students. But Emma didn't want to return. She had a dream, and to accomplish that dream, she knew she had to go on to Madame Marchesi. Stranded on a foreign shore with limited funds, she decided to continue. She telegraphed her father, then courageously proceeded to Vienna alone.

Word circulated through the mining towns of California and Nevada of the Nightingale's troubles. Once again, her old friends came to her aid, sending her enough money to allow her to complete her training.

In Vienna, she faced the famous vocal teacher who had taught other opera singers. Emma sang, the purity of her notes ringing clear, and Madame Marchesi enthusiastically praised her voice and took her on as a pupil. After three years of hard work, Madame

Marchesi pronounced her ready for an official debut. Emma Wixom, who had once pretended she was appearing before royalty by singing to cigar box portraits of Prince Albert and Queen Victoria, made her debut in London at Her Majesty's Theater.

The performance drew praise from even the most skeptical. "A natural coloratura equal to any of her contemporaries," said Sir Thomas Beecham, a conductor who dominated British music for sixty years.

In a review of Emma's first appearance, the *Illustrated London News* complimented her graceful bearing and the "rare power of sustaining an extreme upper note."The review concluded with a comment on the audience response. "Frequent applause and several recalls testified to the complete success of the young debutante, who would seem to have entered on a prosperous career."

Before the performance, Emma had officially taken the stage name of Emma Nevada, explaining in a letter that she wanted to honor the state of Nevada and the city in California where she sang in the Baptist church. In those rugged places, some of the least civilized men in the nation had taken her into their hearts.

As Emma Nevada's career unfolded, opera enthusiasts and critics praised her voice and her stage presence. The languages she'd spent so much time learning at Mills Seminary were now essential, especially so because American singers were looked upon with some disdain by those steeped in generations of Italian, German, and French mastery. Blessed with a natural soprano voice of flutelike purity, she could bring pathos or great sweetness to any role. She sang in various Italian cities; was encouraged by famous composer Guiseppe Verdi, who traveled a thousand miles to see her; joined the Opera Comique in Paris; and did it all with a simple dignity that endeared her to those who saw her.

Unlike other famous entertainers such as Lola Montez (see page 109) and Lotta Crabtree (see page 31), who also started in the gold fields, Emma Nevada was never criticized for a freewheeling lifestyle. In fact, she was praised for her sincerity and pious ways. She joined the Catholic Church while living in Europe, an event remarked upon by a London journal of the time. "Parisian life," it was reported in 1880 by the *London Truth*,

> and above all the life of an actress or singer in Paris, is not supposed to be stimulating in a religious way. But Miss Emma Nevada seems to have had a contrary experience. As the papers have already noticed, she has joined the Catholic Church. The accounts of the French papers are recently to hand. They seem to have taken a great deal of notice of the event, and pronounce it one of the best of the season. The general impression seems to be that Miss Nevada has what we call a very level head and that she has done a remarkably clever thing for her own temporal as well as spiritual welfare.

In late 1884, now a member of the opera company managed by Colonel James Henry Mapleson, Emma returned to America, where she toured as an alternate to "La Diva," Adelina Patti. She was warmly received in New York and even more so in California the next year.

In San Francisco, she once again moved the audience to tears. Someone in the crowded Grand Opera House shouted out a request that Emma sing "Home, Sweet Home." Barely had she begun before her voice broke and tears streamed down her cheeks. She left the stage for a few moments, and when she returned and finished the old favorite, the audience went wild.

The deep emotion that had caused her tears was caused in part by the refusal of Mapleson to let her go home to Austin to visit her family and all her friends there. The tension between the young diva and her manager escalated. He chose all her roles, booked her only in major cities, and then attacked her in a biting interview, saying she was a young prima donna who hadn't yet learned the ropes.

Mapleson was considered an extraordinary character and impresario. He was one of the leading figures in the cultural revolution that brought opera to the raw West. Mapleson ignored criticism and did things his way, generally with great success. However, there were some who denounced Emma's performance in the tragic opera, *Mereille*. Instead of ending on a poignant note as written, a waltz was inserted. This change, Emma said, lifted the spirits of the audience. She agreed that changing the sad ending by reviving her character after death from sunstroke and sending her to the footlights with a waltz was "crazy so far as artistic and dramatic values are concerned," but the general public didn't seem to mind the change. During a two-week engagement in Chicago, Mapleson's company drew almost 100,000 people.

As much as she wanted to return home, Mapleson would not allow it, and she obediently returned to London. There she sang for Queen Victoria and met the man she was to marry. The queen praised her beautiful voice and gracious manner. The young man did more. He courted the singer. Described as a cultivated gentleman, Dr. Raymond Palmer was tall, blue-eyed, and his calm manner reportedly led people to believe him older than the twenty-eight years he claimed at the time.

Rather than a ring to seal their engagement, Palmer gave Emma a bracelet she always treasured. It locked on her arm; the key stayed on his watch chain. Emma Nevada married Dr. Raymond Palmer in Paris on October 1, 1885, a wedding that drew some of the most famous of European society as well as home folks straight from the dry desert of Nevada.

With her husband now managing her career, Emma made another triumphal tour in America. On December 3, 1885, she sang at Piper's Opera House in Virginia City, Nevada and then boarded the train that would take her back to her beloved home in Austin. Bonfires lit up the road up the canyon which marked the final leg of Emma's route. Crowds lined the way, and she blew kisses and waved for the last mile.

Seats for the concert at the Methodist Episcopal Church in Austin had been sold out for days. The *Reese River Reveille* asked that ladies leave their tall hats at home so that everyone would have a chance to see the famous singer. Once again, the "Sagebrush Night-ingale" won an ovation from her audience. It was Emma's last trip to Austin, but it was one the town never forgot.

In 1887, back in Paris, Emma gave birth to a daughter and named her Mignon, after a character in Emma's favorite opera. Years later, Mignon achieved her own fame singing opera in Europe.

Emma herself never forgot her beginnings. In 1902, word of a planned appearance in Nevada City, California spread like wild-fire. Thousands of citizens, farmers, merchants, and miners turned out to see the famous "Queen of the Alpha Diggins," whose career began in Nevada City in a church on the banks of Deer Creek.

Grass Valley cheered as the Nevada County Narrow Gauge Rail-way, fondly dubbed the "Never Come Never Go," brought its fa-mous passenger to the station. Crowds lined the streets as an open carriage carried Emma past the homes on Mill Street where Lola Montez and Lotta Crabtree had lived, then through Grass Valley, over the ridge called Town Talk, past the saloon there, then down into Nevada City and the multitude waiting at the National Hotel.

Her five-foot form nearly dwarfed by the pile of flowers that awaited her on stage, Emma stepped forth and sang. As before, tears flowed freely. Even the blacksmith, Bill Alexander, who had first listened to Emma sing to the tap of his hammer, stood there with handkerchief in hand as he watched the Nightingale perform for those who loved her best.

The applause was thunderous and the tears were heavy the next day as the old Never Come Never Go whistled away from the sta-tion, heading east to Colfax on the shining rails that had briefly returned the beloved singer to her early home.

The love for the Queen of Alpha Diggins never died, despite Emma Nevada's long absences from the shores of America. An hon-orary title was awarded her on her eightieth birthday by the An-cient and Honorable Order of E. Clampus Vitus. The unconventional organization dedicated to preserving California Gold Rush history proclaimed her "Empress of Treasure Island" at the San Francisco Exposition of 1939.

In her letter of thanks, she said she had thought that the state of her birth had forgotten her as new young singers appeared on the scene. "Your letters have made my heart beat with pride and joy, to know that you still have a place for me in your dear California hearts," she wrote.

For twenty-five years her voice had charmed the world, earning the first gold nuggets of the family fortune when she was three. During the last decades of her life, her husband's long illness and the ravages of war dissipated her wealth, but never her spirit. In 1910, she retired from the stage and taught voice technique to students in England.

Emma died at the home of her daughter in Liverpool, England on June 20, 1940. Bombs from the German blitz rained on London during the funeral of "International Songbird" Emma Nevada.

LOLA MONTEZ

Lola Montez

IRISH ADVENTURER

Notorious I have always been and never famous.

Lola Montez
1854

*L*ola stood quietly in the middle of the stage at the Bella Union Saloon in San Francisco and let the audience gaze up at her. She was a captivating beauty with dark, curly hair. Men from the various mining camps around traveled to town nightly to see the "fair-skinned woman with the pretty face." She always began her act the same way:

> Good evening, gentlemen. I am Lola Montez. I was born in the year 1830, in Seville, the capital of Andalucia, the land of the serenades and balconies, of troubadours and romance—the fatherland of Miguel Cervantes, of Las Casas, of the Roman Emperors Trajan and Theodosius.

After the short introduction the music would start and the audience would cheer wildly. Lola would dance out on stage wearing flesh colored tights and a crinoline skirt. The excited crowd didn't know that most of what she had just told them about herself was a lie. Lola had spent so many years creating her fictitious background that she had probably forgotten what the truth was anyway. And as long as the house was packed with men who paid to see her, she didn't care.

Lola was actually born in 1818 in Ireland and her name was really Marie Dolores Eliza Rosanna Gilbert. By the time she had reached the Gold Country in 1851, she had already built a reputation for herself as a woman who possessed extravagant charm and thrived on adventure.

Like many other entertainers, Lola had come to California to enjoy the rewards of the Gold Rush. Stories of gold being tossed at the feet of performers lured many singing and dancing acts west. Lonesome and bored miners had an insatiable appetite for entertainment and they were willing to pay handsomely to see shows and variety acts. Lola Montez became one of the most popular performers of her time.

Lola was well known for a number she called the "Spider Dance." She wore a risqué costume and fluttered around the stage pretending to be trapped inside a spider's web. The music and dance became more and more frantic as giant tarantulas made of cork were dropped down on her from high above the stage. The curious miners were thrilled and shocked at the display. Lola's dancing brought her high praise, but some found the scene a little too provocative for their taste.

On August 22, 1856, a letter to the editor appeared in the *San Francisco Bulletin* describing the effect Lola's jig had on a member of the audience.

> Dear Editor: I've seen considerable dancing in my time, Mr. Editor. I can do a little myself. At a regular 'hoo-down,' I'm hard to beat. But that Spider Dance—Mr. Editor, did you ever see it? There ain't no such dances up our way, nor there wasn't any away off there in Illinois neither. Well, I ain't a married man, yet, but if I was to catch my Sarah Ann a' dancing the Spider Dance I don't think I ever would be either. Yours, Country Joe.

If the course of Lola's life had been left up to her parents she would have settled into a nice stable existence with a sixty-year-old judge of the Supreme Court of India, a marriage her mother and father had arranged for her when she was very young. Lola was wild and restless, and she wanted to see the world. She could not imagine herself married to "a gouty old rascal" or "spending her days rocking by a fire." She defied her family and, at nineteen, ran away from home with a handsome British lieutenant. The two were quickly married. Not long after they had exchanged vows, Lola's husband ran off with another woman. Depressed and lonely, Lola sat down to contemplate the rest of her life. She decided to take up dancing. When she was a little girl, she had been considered an excellent dancer—a natural and a great beauty with an extraordinary gift. She believed it was time to cash in on her talents.

After studying dance in Madrid, she toured Europe. Her debut was held in London in 1847. She was billed as "The Premier Spanish Ballerina." In order to make the act more authentic, she changed her name to Lola Montez, adopted a Spanish accent, and claimed to be of Spanish decent. Audiences adored her. She danced her way into the hearts of Europe and was invited to perform at all its royal courts. Theater critics praised her unique style and charm. In 1847 *The London Telegraph* reported:

> Her figure was even more attractive than her face, lovely as the latter was. Lithe and graceful as a young fawn, every movement that she made seemed filled with melody as she commenced her dance. Her eyes were blazing and flashing with excitement, for she felt that I was prepared to admire her. In her pose, grace seemed involuntarily to preside over her limbs and dispose their attitudes. Her foot and ankle were almost faultless.

Critics, captivated by her provocative dance, had a tendency to exaggerate her abilities. Historical records state that she was only a mediocre dancer, but she excelled at enticing the opposite sex. So intoxicating was her act that even famous, reserved aristocrats were not immune. Lola was always seen with a wealthy gentlemen of considerable position on her arm.

One night when Lola was leaving the theater after a performance, she was greeted at the stage door by the world-famous composer, Franz Liszt. Liszt had seen Lola dance and was swept away by her elegance. She was flattered that he had sought her out and honored that he wanted to spend time with her. The two had a brief affair and historical reports indicate that when Lola ended their relationship, Liszt went through terrible despair. He stayed out of public view while he went through religious turmoil.

Lola also had an affair with author Alexandre Dumas Pere. It is said that he patterned the love interest in his book *The Bride of Monte Cristo* after her. Lola betrayed him with his best friend, journalist Alexander Dujarier. A heartbroken Dumas later wrote that "Lola had an evil eye and would bring a curse on any man who loved her."

While touring Germany in 1847, Lola managed to capture the heart of Ludwig I, King of Bavaria. He was so taken by his new mistress that he showered her with gifts and jewels and gave her the title of Countess of Landsfeld. When Lola was allowed to help the king rule his country, the people of Bavaria were outraged. They rebelled, rioted, chanted slogans condemning Lola, and demanded Ludwig's abdication. Bavarian citizen, Jacob Vennedy, wrote:

> The King of Bavaria wastes the resources of his poor land and the honest sweat of his honorable, persevering subjects on his mistress and their depraved followers. Everyone knows that the jewelry Lola Montez wore recently at the theatre— and this is but a small portion given her by the infatuated King, cost sixty thousand guldens. While this woman revels in her jewels, her fine paintings and her magnificent clothes, the King's loyal subjects plead in vain for a stable government and the chance to earn their living in peace and property. But for the people, nothing is done. Bavaria will not recover from her illness until this woman is sent into exile, never to return.

The propaganda worked, and Lola's influence came to an end. Ludwig lost his crown and Lola was ordered out of the country. In March 1848, Lola left Germany for Switzerland with a strongbox filled with cash and jewels. From there she traveled to Paris to perform in a play written especially for her entitled *Lola Montez in Bavaria.*

When the play ended, Lola returned to London. Her return to England did not create the same amount of attention as it did the first time she was there. European audiences had tired of the Spider Dance, and her popularity began to fade. It seemed her career was over. She was downhearted, penniless, and creditors were now knocking at her door. The life of luxury she had known for so long was gone. She needed to find a way to keep herself adorned in the latest fashions and surrounded by the finer things she had become accustomed to. She quickly accepted a proposal of marriage from a wealthy barrister who promised to take care of her. It wasn't until after the wedding ceremony that she remembered that she was not legally divorced from her first husband. She was now a bigamist and had to leave England to avoid being arrested. She managed to get her first marriage annulled a few months later then decided to divorce her second husband and seek her fortune elsewhere.

Lola felt that the time was right to go to America. She longed to be as well-known there as she was in Europe. The people on this new continent had already heard stories about the Spanish dancer and eagerly awaited her arrival. Theaters in New York, Boston, and Philadelphia were filled with curious citizens all hoping to get a glimpse of the tempestuous Countess of Landsfeld.

Lola had hoped that she could change her image in this new world, but trouble followed her wherever she went. The newspapers covered her dance tour across the country and reported on the fights she had with managers and lovers along the way. Her love for Cuban cigars and exotic birds was the source of many newspaper articles. She was considered quite a spectacle roaming the main streets of various cities and towns smoking a cigar and carrying a white parrot on her shoulder.

Much of the publicity, however, consisted of stories fabricated to keep Lola's name before the public, and it was successful. She always played to packed houses.

Lola and her manager decided California's gold fields held even more promise. Her manager traveled there to secure bookings. Lola followed by ship, and by the time she arrived in San Francisco, she was involved with Patrick Hull, a witty, urbane writer and part owner of a Whig newspaper. He loved her eccentric, wild ways and she thought he was the best storyteller she had ever come across. The two married within a few days of arriving in the booming Bay City.

The newlyweds decided to travel to Grass Valley, California. Grass Valley was a popular mining community and Lola owned shares in a gold mine there. She fell in love with the area. She said it reminded her of her home in Bavaria. She stunned her husband and manager when she announced that she was hanging up her dancing shoes and setting up house in this small town. She bought a home on Mill Street and furnished it with lavish decorations including costly carpets and a zinc bathtub. Outside she had a magnificent rose garden and a menagerie of animals: canaries, dogs, sheep, a goat, a horse, a wildcat, a parrot, a lamb, and a grizzly bear. Dignitaries and important personalities from all over the world came to visit her. Because most of these visitors were male, Lola was the source of many rumors. Those rumors were further fueled when an article in *Harper's Weekly Reporter* revealed a dark secret from Lola's past.

> Lola and I talked frankly about many things on our walks
> and rides together through the hills. What bothered her most
> was being called a whore by people who believed all the lies
> that were written about her. She told me she never earned
> her living as a prostitute except for one short period, and she
> wasn't ashamed to admit it.

By this time, Lola's marriage to Hull was suffering. He was a dedicated newsman and he missed his paper. He wanted to move back to San Francisco. Lola insisted on staying in Grass Valley. The two fought constantly. Their arguments were loud and violent. One of their fights about leaving the area ended with Lola throwing Patrick's suitcase out of the window. Hull went back to the paper and Lola filed for divorce, proclaiming to everyone that she was tired of "Hully wedlock" anyway.

A scathing article criticizing Lola for divorcing Patrick and for her lack of morals appeared in the *Grass Valley Telegraph.* She became furious with the editor of the paper, Henry Shipley, for printing the piece. She charged out of her home with the offending paper in one hand and a riding whip in the other. She hurried over to the Golden Gate Saloon, ran right up to Shipley who was seated at the bar, and attempted to hit him over the head with her whip. He grabbed her arm and jerked the whip away from her. She demanded that he apologize for printing the article. He refused. Lola asked the miners at the bar to help her, but they just laughed. Not even her promise of a free drink prompted them to come to her assistance. She left the saloon humiliated.

She later wrote that she was forced to use her riding whip, which had never been used on the back of a horse, to whip an "Ass." She was so humiliated by the incident that she went into seclusion for a short time.

Lola left Grass Valley in 1855 to return to the stage. But this time, Lola and her manager miscalculated. Her return to the new Metropolitan theater ended in disaster. Her manager next persuaded her to tour Australia. Again, things didn't go as well as they hoped. Authorities in several cities branded the Spider Dance immoral and refused to allow its performance. A Methodist minister who condemned the dance as well as the dancer got more than he expected when his comments got back to Lola. She was so angry that she stomped over to his home, threw off her coat, and performed her dance in costume before the shocked man and his wife. He never again mentioned the flamboyant dancer to his congregation.

With the costly failure of the Australian tour, Lola was hard-pressed to get herself and her troupe back to America. Once reported to be wealthy, Lola was now down to her last reserves. She charmed a ship's captain into giving her and her crew tickets on a boat bound for San Francisco. The trip was a difficult one. Her manager was so upset about the failure of Lola's tour that he threw himself overboard. Lola was devastated. She sold her house in Grass Valley and retired from the stage.

In 1859, she returned to New York where she made a living giving how-to-keep-your-beauty lectures. Grace Greenwood, a leading female correspondent, reported that she found Lola's lectures even "more demoralizing that her dancing." A year later, Lola retired, and, using the name Mrs. Fanny Gibbons, settled in the Prospect Park section of Brooklyn. There she suffered a stroke and was left unable to speak.

News of her identity and pitiful condition hit the newspapers. The stories brought an old acquaintance to see her. Mrs. Isaac Buchanan promised to take care of her and moved her into the Buchanan home. Lola deeded over all her possessions to the women she saw as a benefactor, but a few days later, her heartless rescuer installed her in a tenement bedroom in an area later known as Hell's Kitchen. Lola Montez died there, unrecognized and alone in January, 1861. She was forty-two. The epitaph on her gravestone in the Greenwood Cemetery in Brooklyn simply reads: Mrs. Eliza Gilbert.

Afterword

Avast, invisible network links the past and the present. It is a network that can be reduced to business documents, personal journals, and newspaper records, but those artifacts are merely the results of the workings of the network.

Of more importance is something harder to define and impossible to hold in hand. It is the spirit, the imagination, and the will of the people who took the first step on an unknown trail. It is the connections those people made, one to another to another, that resulted in the shape of our lives today. It is the helping hand offered and the sharing of stories and songs around a campfire or in a candle-lit parlor or meeting hall. It is as much the gathering of a community to build a school or a church as it is the building of a railroad connecting east and west.

The years of the California Gold Rush are unparalleled in American history. If you could dump into a gold pan the two years between the discovery of gold in 1848 and the granting of statehood in 1850, you would find many solid nuggets of achievement amidst the heavy black sands of injustice and ignorance.

Terrible consequences followed as men rushed to California to scoop up a fortune. Diseases wiped out untold thousands of Native Americans who had lived for centuries in a sustainable universe. The landscape was radically altered as forests were cut and replaced by towns and gold mines, both often surrounded by huge piles of waste rock.

People brought more than dreams of better things to the wilderness. They also brought their prejudices and narrow codes of conduct. Juanita's story might not have ended with a rope had the participants been more tolerant. Mary Hallock Foote might have written a Pulitzer quality book instead of supplying the raw materials for one. Madame Mustache might have married her true love instead of a man who left her penniless a month after the wedding. As these stories show, sometimes the will and the spirit were not enough to overcome the legacies of ignorance, prejudice, and greed of some of those who came west for a better life.

A glimpse of the network that links the past and the future can be felt when visiting one of the gold rush towns along California's Highway 49, which links the southern mines to their northern counterparts. In places like Bodie, the preserved ghost town and state historic park, the utter isolation, the wind, the silence, provide a taste of the way it was.

Archives and museums display artifacts of the unseen network, but it is the personal histories of the people who forged a new life with their bare hands in order to provide a better future for their families that links us all together. Who we are today is in part a result of our ancestors' dreams and ambitions. It behooves us all to dream well of the future.

Bibliography

General References

Archer, W. H. *History of the Development of Anesthesia.* Pittsburgh, 1971.

Jensen, Jean and Gloria Lothrop. *California Women: A History.* San Francisco: Boyd and Fraser Publishing, 1987.

Levy, JoAnn. *They Saw the Elephant.* Hamden, Conn.: Archon, 1990.

Margo, Elizabeth. *Women of the Gold Rush: Taming the Forty-Niner.* New York: Indian Head Books, 1955.

Maury, F. *Treatises on the Dental Art.* 1843. Reprint, Boston: Milford House, 1972.

Neville, Amelia Ransome. *The Fantastic City: Memoirs of the Social and Romantic Life of Old San Francisco.* Virginia Brastow. Ed. Boston: Houghton Mifflin, 1932.

Sacher, Susan, ed. *Hypatia's Sisters, Biographies of Women Scientists Past and Present.* Seattle: Feminists North West, 1976.

Nancy Kelsey

Farquhar, Francis P. *History of Sierra Nevada.* Berkeley and Los Angeles: University of California Press, 1965.

Lardner, W. B. and M. J. Brock. *History of Placer and Nevada County.* Los Angeles: Historic Record Company, 1924.

Sherman, D. "A California Heroine." *San Francisco Examiner.* February 5, 1893.

Mary Graves

Bancroft, Hubert Howe. *Annals of the California Gold Era.* Berkeley: The Bancroft Company, 1918.

Foley, D. "Heroine of the Donner Party." Nevada County Historical Society Bulletin. August 3, 1964.

McGlashan, C. F. *History of the Donner Party.* Stanford, Calif.: Stanford University Press, 1940.

Stewart, George R. *Ordeal by Hunger.* New York: Henry Holt & Company, 1936.

Lotta Crabtree

Dempsy, David and Raymond R. Baldwin. *Triumph of Lotta Crabtree*. New York: William Morrow & Company, Inc. 1968.

DeNevi, Donald P. *Sketches of California*. San Francisco: Chronicle Books, 1937.

Lockridge, Richard. *Darling of Misfortune*. New York: The Century Company, 1932.

Rourke, Constance. *Troupers of the Gold Coast*. San Francisco: Harcourt, Brace & Company, 1928.

Seagraves, Ann. *Women of the Sierra*. Lakeport, Calif.: Wesanne Enterprises, 1990.

Eliza Withington

Mason, Jesse. *History of Amador County* (microfilm). New Haven Research Publications, 1967.

Myres, Sandra L., ed. "Journal of Mary Stuart Bailey." In *Ho for California! Women's Overland Diaries*. San Marino, Calif.: Huntington Library, 1980.

Newhall, Beaumont. *History of Photography 1839 to Present Day*. Boston: Little, Brown, 1982.

Palmquist, Peter. *California History*. Spring, 1992.

Palmquist, Peter. *Shadowcatchers, A Directory of Women in California Photography before 1901*. Arcata: P.E. Palmquist, 1990.

Rosenblum, Naomi. *History of Women Photographers*. Paris; N.Y.: Abbeville Press, 1994.

Volcano Ledger. July, 1857.

Eleanora Dumont

Johnson, Russ and Anne. *The Ghost Town of Bodie*. Bishop, Calif.: Sierra Media, 1967.

Nash, Robert J. *Encyclopedia of Western Lawmen & Outlaws*. Los Angeles: First Paragon House 1989.

Paine, Bob. "Madame Moustache—A Glimpse of History." *The Mountain Messenger,* December 9, 1982.

Perkins, William. *Memoirs of William Perkins*. University of California, Berkeley: Perkins Books, 1893.

Thompson, H. and Albert H. West. *History of Nevada County, California.* Oakland, Calif.: Howell–North, 1880.

Williams III, George. *The Red Light Ladies of Virginia City.* Riverside, Calif.: Tree By The River Publishing, 1984.

Luzena Stanley Wilson

Alta California News. August, 1858.

DeNevi, Don. *Sketches of Early California.* San Francisco: Chronicle, 1971.

Schlissel, Lillian. *Women's Diaries of the Westward Journey.* New York: Schocken Books, 1982.

Juanita

Barstow, D. "Witness." *Alta California News.* August 4, 1851.

Buck, Franklin. "Juanita." *Pacific Star. Steamer Edition.* July 15, 1851.

McClosky, J. .J. "Josefa." *San Jose Pioneer.* November 12, 1881.

Seagraves, Ann. *Women of the Sierra.* Lakeport, Calif.: Wesanne Enterprises, 1990.

Secrest, William B. *Juanita.* Fresno, Calif.: Saga–West Publishing Company, 1967.

Ellen Sargent

Anthony, Katherine. *Susan B. Anthony, Her Personal History and Her Era.* Garden City, Calif.: Doubleday, 1954.

Daily Alta California. November 10, 1869, and September 18, 1879.

Davis, Rita. *California Women, a Guide to Their Politics 1885–1911.* San Francisco: California Scene, 1967.

Freeman, Christine. "Aaron Augustus Sargent; Nevada County's International Citizen." *Nevada County Historical Society Bulletin.* July, 1978.

Moynihan, Ruth Barnes. *Abigail "Rebel for Rights" Scott Duniway.* New Haven: Yale University Press, 1983.

San Diego Union. August 15, 1877.

San Francisco Call. July 26, 1911.

San Francisco Chronicle. June 22, 1904.

Stanton, Elizabeth. *History of Woman Suffrage Volume VIII.* New York: Source Book Press, 1970.

Nellie Pooler Chapman

A. E. Chapman letter. September 28, 1892. *Dental Register of the West.* San Francisco, 1858.

Daily Bee. December 24, 1880.

"Full History of the Destruction of Nevada by Fire on the 19th of July." *Daily Alta California.* August 8, 1856.

Hartman, Dr. Berthal J. *Dentistry and the University of California.* San Francisco: University of California San Francisco Press, 1997.

Kiley, Bill. *Sierra Heritage.* November/December, 1992.

The Union. Grass Valley, CA. March 6, 1984.

Van der Pas, Peter W. "The Chapman Family of Nevada City." *Nevada County Historical Society Bulletin.* October 1990.

Mary Hallock Foote

Browne, Juanita. "The Illustrator Was a Lady." *Sierra Heritage.* January/February, 1990.

Erisman, Fred, and Richard Etulain. *Fifty Western Writers.* Westwood, Conn: Greenwood Press, 1982.

Etulain, Richard. *Conversations with Wallace Stegner.* Salt Lake City: University of Utah Press, 1983.

Lardner, William. *History of Placer and Nevada Counties.* Los Angeles: Historic Record Company, 1924.

Letters of Mary Hallock Foote. Courtesy of The Huntington Library, Art Collections and Botanical Gardens. San Marino, Calif.

Maguire, James H. *Mary Hallock Foote. Western Writers Series.* Boise, Idaho: Boise State College, 1972.

Foote, Mary Hallock. Rodman Paul, editor. *A Victorian Gentlewoman in the Far West.* San Marino, Calif.: The Huntington Library, 1980.

Emma Nevada

Argonaut. April 26, 1884.

Busch, Hans. Translator. *Verdi's "Otello" and "Simon Boccanegra" in Letters and Documents.* Oxford: Clarendon Press, 1988.

Hunt, Rockwell. "Emma Nevada 'The Comstock Nightingale.'" *California Stately Hall of Fame.* Stockton: College of the Pacific, 1950.

Illustrated London News. May 22, 1880.

Kent, Genevieve. *Nevada County Historical Society Bulletin.* Nevada City, Calif., July 1951.

Leigh, R. W. Nevada. *The Silver State; Lander Co.* Carson City: Western States Historical Publishers, 1970.

Nevada State Journal. November 7, 1954, and March 1, 1954.

New York Times. June 22, 1940.

Oakland Tribune. June 30, 1940.

Sacramento Bee. June 22, 1940.

Truth. London, England. March 11, 1880, and May 20 1880.

Lola Montez

Callahan, Bob. "William Kennedy and the Ghost of Lola Montez." *Image Magazine.* Sunday, August 28, 1988.

Darling, Amanda. *Lola Montez.* New York: Stein & Day, 1972.

Holdredge, Helen. *The Woman In Black.* New York: Putnam Books, 1955.

Thompson, H. and Albert A. West. *History of Nevada County, California.* Oakland, Calif.: Howell–North Books, 1880.

Wydnham, Horace. *Magnificent Montez.* New York: Hillman Curl, 1937.

Index

Index

About the Authors

JoAnn Chartier is an artist and writer living in California's historic Gold Rush Country. She has worked as both a print and broadcast journalist and as a talk show host, devoting many programs to historical themes. Her work in broadcast media has won awards; she is co-author and producer of an audio tape telling the stories of historic sites, and of a series of historical minutes for use on radio.

Chris Enss is a standup comic and comedy writer with an extensive background in radio and television. Her educational background includes studies in journalism and cinematography. She has sold six screenplays to various Hollywood production companies and is currently working on another comic feature film. Her hobbies are historical research and writing about women of the Old West.